Michael Shernoff, MSW
Editor

Gay Widowers
Life After the Death
of a Partner

Gay Widowers: Life After the Death of a Partner has been co-published simultaneously as *Journal of Gay & Lesbian Social Services,* Volume 7, Number 2 1997.

Pre-publication
REVIEWS,
COMMENTARIES,
EVALUATIONS . . .

"**V**entures into the barely explored, but sadly all-too-familiar terrain of gay men's grief. . . . Taken separately, these memoirs overflow with homespun eloquence and wisdom. Together, they weave into something larger–a powerful mosaic reflecting the diversity and breadth of our communal loss, the depth of our resilience."

Steven Schwartzberg, PhD
Assistant Clinical Professor
of Psychology
Department of Psychiatry
Harvard Medical School

More pre-publication
REVIEWS, COMMENTARIES, EVALUATIONS . . .

"With his signature blend of professional integrity, modesty and economy of literary expression, boldness of purpose, and clarity of vision, Shernoff leads us through one of the most revealing and cathartic books to emerge from the interface of literature and the healing arts. . . . A landmark collection–ostensibly about a very depressing subject–that leads us to a place of joyful transcendence through the same simple process that writing at its best has always utilized–telling the truth, in all its messiness, of where we've been, how much it has hurt, of the mistakes we've made, of the love we've known."

Lawrence D. Mass, Co-Founder
Gay Men's Health Crisis, New York, NY
Author: Confessions of a Jewish Wagnerite: Being Gay and Jewish in America; *Editor:* Dialogues of the Sexual Revolution, Volumes I and II *and of* We Must Love One Another or Die: The Life and Legacies of Larry Kramer

"Bears witness to the realities of 'gay widowhood,' a neglected and often denied phenomenon. Making use of vivid and inspiring firsthand narratives, the book presents very private views of the raw emotions of gay men who have lived through the loss of their partners. . . . Shernoff highlights the diversity of psychological reactions and coping styles in the bereavement and developmental processes and expertly normalizes and validates the range of experiences of this group of men."

Robert H. Remien, PhD
Clinical Psychologist/Research Scientist, The HIV Center for Clinical and Behavioral Studies at the New York State Psychiatric Institute and Columbia University

The Harrington Park Press

Gay Widowers:
Life After the Death
of a Partner

Gay Widowers: Life After the Death of a Partner has been co-published simultaneously as *Journal of Gay & Lesbian Social Services,* Volume 7, Number 2 1997.

Gay Widowers:
Life After the Death
of a Partner

Michael Shernoff, MSW
Editor

Gay Widowers: Life After the Death of a Partner, edited by Michael Shernoff, was simultaneously issued by The Haworth Press, Inc., under the same title, as a special issue of the *Journal of Gay & Lesbian Social Services*, Volume 7, Number 2, 1997, James J. Kelly, Editor.

The Harrington Park Press
An Imprint of
The Haworth Press, Inc.
New York • London

ISBN 1-56023-105-X

Published by

The Harrington Park Press, 10 Alice Street, Binghamton, NY 13904-1580 USA

The Harrington Park Press is an imprint of The Haworth Press, Inc., 10 Alice Street, Binghamton, NY 13904-1580 USA.

Gay Widowers: Life After the Death of a Partner has been co-published simultaneously as *Journal of Gay & Lesbian Social Services*, Volume 7, Number 2 1997.

The development, preparation, and publication of this work has been undertaken with great care. However, the publisher, employees, editors, and agents of The Haworth Press and all imprints of The Haworth Press, Inc., including The Haworth Medical Press and The Pharmaceutical Products Press, are not responsible for any errors contained herein or for consequences that may ensue from use of materials or information contained in this work. Opinions expressed by the author(s) are not necessarily those of The Haworth Press, Inc.

Cover design by Thomas J. Mayshock Jr.
Cover photo: 1988 San Francisco Lesbian and Gay Freedom Day Parade. Courtesy of Allan Berube (photographer unknown)

Library of Congress Cataloging-in-Publication Data

Gay widowers : life after the death of a partner / Michael Shernoff, editor.
     p. cm.
     Originally published in the Journal of gay & lesbian social services, v. 7, no. 2, 1997.
     Includes bibliographical references and index.
     ISBN 0-7890-0355-4 (hc). -- ISBN 1-56023-105-X (sc)
     1. Gay men–United States–Psychology. 2. Widowers–United States–Psychology. 3. Bereavement–United States. 4. Gay male couples–United States. I. Shernoff, Michael, 1951- . II. Journal of gay & lesbian social services, v. 7, no. 2.

HQ76.2.U5G398 1997
305.38'9664–dc21
                                               97-33478
                                                 CIP

It is with the profoundest love, respect and joy that I dedicate this book to the following two individuals:

Philip Glennon Ryan, my first love, my first husband and now my life long friend.

Dr. Ellen Siroka-Robinson, mentor, guide and sorceress whose patience and perseverence has helped me transform my life, attain a sense of myself and a belief in all that I am capable of while continuously improving upon and savoring all aspects of my wondrous journey.

INDEXING & ABSTRACTING

Contributions to this publication are selectively indexed or abstracted in print, electronic, online, or CD-ROM version(s) of the reference tools and information services listed below. This list is current as of the copyright date of this publication. See the end of this section for additional notes.

- *AIDS Newsletter c/o CAB International/CAB ACCESS . . . available in print, diskettes updated weekly, and on INTERNET. Providing full bibliographic listings, author affiliation, augmented keyword searching,* CAB International, P.O. Box 100,Wallingford Oxon OX10 8DE, United Kingdom

- *Cambridge Scientific Abstracts, Risk Abstracts,* 7200 Wisconsin Avenue #601, Bethesda, MD 20814

- *caredata CD: the social and community care database,* National Institute for Social Work, 5 Tavistock Place, London WC1H 9SS, England

- *CNPIEC Reference Guide: Chinese National Directory of Foreign Periodicals,* P.O. Box 88, Beijing, People's Republic of China

- *Criminal Justice Abstracts,* Willow Tree Press, 15 Washington Street, 4th Floor, Newark, NJ 07102

- *Digest of Neurology and Psychiatry,* The Institute of Living, 400 Washington Street, Hartford, CT 06106

- *ERIC Clearinghouse on Urban Education (ERIC/CUE),* Teachers College, Columbia University, Box 40, New York, NY 10027

- *Family Studies Database (online and CD/ROM),* National Information Services Corporation, 306 East Baltimore Pike, 2nd Floor, Media, PA 19063

- *HOMODOK/"Relevant" Bibliographic Database,* Documentation Centre for Gay & Lesbian Studies, University of Amsterdam (selective printed abstracts in "Homologie" and bibliographic computer databases covering cultural, historical, social and political aspects of gay & lesbian topics), c/o HOMODOK-ILGA Archive, O. Z. Achterburgwal 185, NL-1012 DK, Amsterdam, The Netherlands

(continued)

- *IBZ International Bibliography of Periodical Literature,* Zeller Verlag GmbH & Co., P.O.B. 1949, d-49009 Osnabruck, Germany

- *Index to Periodical Articles Related to Law,* University of Texas, 727 East 26th Street, Austin, TX 78705

- *INTERNET ACCESS (& additional networks) Bulletin Board for Libraries ("BUBL"), coverage of information resources on INTERNET, JANET, and other networks.*
  - <URL:http://bubl.ac.uk/>
  - The new locations will be found under <URL:http://bubl.ac. uk/link/>.
  - Any existing BUBL users who have problems finding information on the new service should contact the BUBL help line by sending e-mail to <bubl@bubl.ac.uk>.
  The Andersonian Library, Curran Building, 101 St. James Road, Glasgow G4 0NS, Scotland

- *Mental Health Abstracts (online through DIALOG),* IFI/Plenum Data Company, 3202 Kirkwood Highway, Wilmington, DE 19808

- *Referativnyi Zhurnal (Abstracts Journal of the Institute of Scientific Information of the Republic of Russia),* The Institute of Scientific Information, Baltijskaja ul., 14, Moscow A-219, Republic of Russia

- *Social Work Abstracts,* National Association of Social Workers, 750 First Street NW, 8th Floor, Washington, DC 20002

- *Sociological Abstracts (SA),* Sociological Abstracts, Inc., P.O. Box 22206, San Diego, CA 92192-0206

- *Studies on Women Abstracts,* Carfax Publishing Company, P.O. Box 25, Abingdon, Oxon OX14 3UE, United Kingdom

- *Violence and Abuse Abstracts: A Review of Current Literature on Interpersonal Violence (VAA),* Sage Publications, Inc., 2455 Teller Road, Newbury Park, CA 91320

(continued)

SPECIAL BIBLIOGRAPHIC NOTES

related to special journal issues (separates)
and indexing/abstracting

☐ indexing/abstracting services in this list will also cover material in any "separate" that is co-published simultaneously with Haworth's special thematic journal issue or DocuSerial. Indexing/abstracting usually covers material at the article/chapter level.

☐ monographic co-editions are intended for either non-subscribers or libraries which intend to purchase a second copy for their circulating collections.

☐ monographic co-editions are reported to all jobbers/wholesalers/approval plans. The source journal is listed as the "series" to assist the prevention of duplicate purchasing in the same manner utilized for books-in-series.

☐ to facilitate user/access services all indexing/abstracting services are encouraged to utilize the co-indexing entry note indicated at the bottom of the first page of each article/chapter/contribution.

☐ this is intended to assist a library user of any reference tool (whether print, electronic, online, or CD-ROM) to locate the monographic version if the library has purchased this version but not a subscription to the source journal.

☐ individual articles/chapters in any Haworth publication are also available through the Haworth Document Delivery Service (HDDS).

CONTENTS

ALL HARRINGTON PARK PRESS BOOKS
ARE PRINTED ON CERTIFIED
ACID-FREE PAPER

ABOUT THE EDITOR

Michael Shernoff, MSW, is a psychotherapist in private practice in Manhattan and is adjunct faculty at Hunter College Graduate School of Social Work. He founded and was Co-Director of Chelsea Psychotherapy Associates until December 1993. He is Editor of *Counseling Chemically Dependent People with HIV Illness* and *Human Services for Gay People: Clinical and Community Practice* and Co-Editor of *The Sourcebook on Lesbian/Gay Health Care, Volumes I and II* and *The Second Decade of AIDS: A Mental Health Practice Handbook.* Also a contributor to the 19th Edition of the *Encyclopedia of Social Work,* he is currently a Contributing Editor of *In the Family* magazine and Senior Consulting Editor of the *Journal of Gay & Lesbian Social Services* (The Haworth Press, Inc.). Mr. Shernoff co-authored three of the most widely used AIDS prevention interventions for gay and bisexual men as well as three brochures and over 30 articles on AIDS prevention and mental health issues pertaining to lesbians and gay men.

A former board member of the National Lesbian/Gay Health Foundation, he served on the National Association of Social Workers National Committee on Lesbian and Gay Issues from 1986 until 1989. He has co-chaired the AIDS Task Force for both the Society for the Scientific Study of Sex and the American Orthopsychiatric Association. Mr. Shernoff welcomes reader correspondence and can be reached by e-mail at: mshernoff@aol.com or on his home page on the World Wide Web at: http://members.aol.com/therapysvc.

*For one human being
to love another . . .
That is perhaps the
most difficult of
all our tasks, the
final and ultimate proof,
the task for which all
others are but
preparation.*

–R. Maria Rilke

*Grief is madness–ask anyone who's been there. They will tell you it abates
with time, but that's a lie. What drowns you in the first year is a force
of solitude and helplessness exactly equal in intensity to the love you had
for the one who's gone. Equally passionate, equally intimate. The spaces between
the stabs of pain grow longer after a while, but they're empty spaces. The
cliches of condolence get you back to the office, back to your taxes and the dinner
table–and for everyone else's sake, you collaborate. The road of least
resistance is paved with the gravel of well-meaning friends,
rather like the gravel that cremation leaves.*

–Paul Monette, *Last Watch of the Night*, 1994

Foreword

Two months after Lee's death, Michael leaned across the table and said to me, "Initially I didn't even know if he was turned on to me. I knew I was attracted to him, but it wasn't until after dinner, when I suggested that we get dessert and bring it back to my place, that I began to flirt with the idea of possibly having sex with Dennis." I thought to myself, "It's not that long since Lee died, but this seems right."

"Well," I asked, "Did you?"

"I did," Michael said. Then, "When did you begin to feel you were ready for that kind of date?"

"Oh, for me, it was very different," I answered. "The problem wasn't the first date. The problem for me was the first person who slept over the whole night."

"Isn't it always different," Michael said. "Different, and complicated. With no rules and no one to rely on for advice. It's a brand new world out there. And we've got no idea what we're doing, do we?"

That—or something close to it—was part of a discussion I had with the editor of this book, crucial to this book coming into being. The details of being widowers had come up between us not long before at a New Year's Day party, partly because we were talking about the

---

Felice Picano is the author of 16 books, including the international best sellers *The Lure*, *The New Joy of Gay Sex* (with Charles Silverstein), and *Like People in History*. He is the winner of the 1996 Ferro-Grumley Award, and his third volume of memoirs, *A House on the Ocean, A House on the Bay* was published in 1997.

[Haworth co-indexing entry note]: "Foreword." Picano, Felice. Co-published simultaneously in *Journal of Gay & Lesbian Social Services* (The Haworth Press, Inc.) Vol. 7, No. 2, 1997, pp. xvii-xxiv; and: *Gay Widowers: Life After the Death of a Partner* (ed: Michael Shernoff) The Haworth Press, Inc., 1997, pp. xiii-xx; and: *Gay Widowers: Life After the Death of a Partner* (ed: Michael Shernoff) The Harrington Park Press, an imprint of The Haworth Press, Inc., 1997, pp. xiii-xx. Single or multiple copies of this article are available for a fee from The Haworth Document Delivery Service [1-800-342-9678, 9:00 a.m. - 5:00 p.m. (EST). E-mail address: getinfo@haworth.com].

host of the party, a mutual friend, who, like us, had lost the man closest to him in his life. In our friend's case, the effect had not been the carefully released grief and cautious moving onward with his life, which Michael had exhibited, nor was it my deep depression and years of reassessment, but instead a tremendous blossoming: he'd redecorated his apartment, begun traveling around the world, become an art-collector, put together a new circle of friends, physically altered himself for the better, became healthier and was even engaging in amateur theatricals: an altogether unexpected transformation.

We naturally talked about him, and about others we knew who had all lost a lover, a close friend, a group of friends, a social network, or for that matter an entire community through AIDS and other causes over the past decade—and how each of us had undergone different kinds of transformations as we moved from being part of a unit, couple, a group, into being a single person again: one barely recognized by society in general, or for that matter given more than lip service by what was left of our community—very often a person we ourselves no longer recognized, so changed were we by life experiences—especially the AIDS epidemic.

Some of these changes are from being a part of something larger to being solitary again had been easy, the stages along the way evident. Others were difficult with more subterranean and shadowy alterations taking place. Michael pinpointed the source of many differences responsible for how we'd changed—the circumstances surrounding our loved one's deaths. In each case, we had been the primary care-giver, the single person he had most turned to, and increasingly relied upon as illness dominated his life, then as his life ended.

As we began comparing details of our experiences with each other, we'd ask each other questions: what did I and my partner do about medical power of attorney and did it work? How did Michael and Lee handle financial and legal matters while Lee was ill? What were Lee's parents and family like when he was dying and afterward? What role and effects—positive and negative—did Bob's employees and law partner have while he was dying? It turned out that Lee was not afraid of death, believed in some sort of afterlife, and thus he and Michael had easily and in some detail, been able to discuss his dying when the time was appropriate, easing both of their minds. Bob, on the other hand, wasn't sure of an afterlife. He was afraid of dying, and my daily attempts at reconciling Bob to his death were daily unraveled by Bob's mother, herself afraid of death and of losing her only son.

For Michael, a major problem had been Lee's dementia in the months before his death. Few gay men are unaware of this problem so prevalent among those with AIDS, and many approach it with great fearfulness: it can be extremely upsetting to lose such a basic assumed ability as control over one's mind. We spoke in some detail of how that had manifested in Lee and of the stages the two had gone through, not only of Lee's dementia but of Michael's process in coming to deal with it, from anger and frustration to acceptance. We compared it to how dementia had manifested in my younger brother and in my business partner, and how differently the requirements and responses had been with each individual.

It soon became obvious we'd had very different experiences with loved ones, but since Michael is a therapist working out of Chelsea, in Manhattan–one of the Ground Zeroes of the AIDS epidemic–he also had many work-related cases of sickness and death, and of widowerhood, to compare to his own experience. As middle-aged gay men in New York, we both found that over the years we'd watched and been near to a great many people dying. As a result we had the dubious distinction of having amassed an entire range of experiences, and enormous amounts of material not only from the many friends and lovers whose deaths we'd been close to–but from those we'd heard about.

The same matters and concerns seemed to come up time and time again as the dying process played itself out, and then was followed by funerals, memorials and widowerhood. And they weren't only seen in gay men and their friends. This past Spring, a divorced straight friend, very estranged from his wife and her new partner, was losing a four year old son to leukemia and he turned to me because he knew I was so experienced.

During this friend's most panicky time, when it became clear to an objective outsider that the child was dying, I had written out a short list. Afterward the young father said how useful that list had been: partly because it reminded him that he wasn't alone–someone he knew well had gone through the same kind of thing—partly because the list was practical. While it contained nothing to comfort him, it also showed he had nothing to fear but the facts themselves. "You saved my life," he later told me. "All around me people were saying the most ridiculous bull shit that I wanted to punch them out, then I'd look at your list and read: 'You are not in control of your son's life. You have only limited responsibility for it. Keep this in mind at all times,' and I'd stop hitting myself over the head and calm down and do something for him."

Meanwhile another friend, a woman who'd been living without marrying a man for over fifteen years, came home from work to find her partner had died of a stroke. A successful business woman who always planned ahead, she found many of the problems that faced her now were completely unprecedented. While she'd been able to foresee and prepare for larger problems such as co-owner-ship of their home and funds, she found herself stymied at every turn by smaller things, by paperwork, by governmental agencies, funeral homes, even the church and graveyard where he was bu-ried—all of whom made it clear they preferred dealing with a rela-tive, even a distant one who'd not seen her partner in forty years, than with her. This is an experience shared by many gay men who have lost their partners. Her frustration was great but more so was her realization of how out of the mainstream the two of them had been living and at what eventual price.

So we knew we were by no means the only people undergoing these intense loss experiences, but we also knew that for us as gay men in the 90s, there were distinctive problems to cope with. To begin with our own situation was relatively new. Up to quite recent-ly, one partner would die of AIDS and within a year or two his partner would also usually die. Whatever period of loss he experi-enced would often be dominated by his own health problems and by involvement in his own dying.

Then there is the larger question connected with being gay and surviving a partner's death being a completely unique societal situa-tion. Our heterosexual grandmothers and grandfathers had been handed down certain traditional social rules for how to be a widow, how to be a widower. And along with those rules, a certain status, a place in society to compensate for their loss. Our parents have taken this and modified and updated it somewhat, retaining the status. But grieving gay men—some of whom have only recently come to think of themselves as adults even though they've gone through so much already—have no rules to follow, no advice, no models—and certainly no compensations of status. Without the approval, or even recognition of our plight by most of society, we seem doomed to individually thrash our way through our individual darkness. We and thousands like us.

Clearly some sort of guide is needed. Not for the dying, not even for the grieving process: there are already guides for that, but simply for gay men whose partners have died. Though this book was born out of AIDS deaths, it became apparent that gay men had no guides or resources to turn to no matter what their partner died from. Thus Michael felt it was important that this book transcend AIDS and become more universal by allowing the voices of as many gay men whose lovers had died of what ever cause to be heard.

The conversation between Michael and I over the lunch during which this book took form confirmed something I had come to experience quite solidly: in our society, you are a widow, or widower, for about a year. During that year, you—even some gay men—are granted all sorts of appropriate rights and sensitivities. Once that year or so is over, so is your special status. Yet we discovered that it is exactly at this point in the process when the greatest and most difficult problems often begin for most of us who have lost a long-term partner. And it's worse when, as with many gay men and lesbians lately, you are involved in a period of recurring loss, losing a partner/lover, then a friend, another lover, another old friend, etc.

Death, like life, is a process. And it is a process you share with your loved one. It is not divided into discrete little chunks as many attempt to outline it; it is a continuous process, which begins the moment that you half-consciously accept the probability that you are about to lose someone very close to you; this process may not end until years, even many years, later.

During the course of our conversation Michael and I discussed that widowerhood more or less occurs in three phases, only one of which is the societally accepted year or so of grief after you've lost your partner. We saw that as merely the middle period, which is flanked on one side by a period of widowerhood in which your companion is still alive, and on the other side by a period of widowerhood long after he is dead.

During the first phase your partner is still alive, and the actual mourning and grieving begins as the process of widowerhood commences with the various losses his illness starts to impose on your life as your relationship changes from an equal partnership into an unequal dependency. This is almost always overlooked by you and others due to an unusual amount of external distraction caused by your changing circumstances–i.e., having to deal with so many new things: hospitals, labs, doctors, social workers, sometimes ambulances, police, lawyers and various business and governmental bureaucracies–and by the enormous amounts of new data and techniques you have to quickly assimilate and learn just to keep step with what's going on. It is crucial to realize, however, that at this moment you two are being forced to renegotiate your partnership contract.

At the same time, something subtle, even insidious, is occurring: you are learning to deal with him being gone. And if you doubt that, speak to anyone whose loved one has for the very first time left home with some minor symptom of AIDS requiring a short stay in the hospital. The fear and panic–or denial and frozen emotions–these first week-long hospitalizations can cause may seem to others to be greatly exaggerated overreactions. Instead, they are often healthy, containing as they do recognitions of the future of the person about to be widowered.

The second phase we all know about, and it remains striking and crucial because your loss is so obvious and complete to yourself and everyone else. It too has its dangers and hidden downfalls. The support network that had become so useful during your loved one's death is often suddenly removed at this stage. People you've come to rely on vanish, thinking there's no need for themselves in your life. Others, hoping to help you, or perhaps feeling guilty about your loss and their helplessness, attempt to push you through your grieving at an unreasonable speed. Others attempt to pull you into a constant chain of social events and distractions, saying that this is so you won't stay home and mope. This doesn't recognize your special need to be alone more than before, partly to rest from the mental, emotional and sometimes physical exertions you've just gone through, sometimes just for you to try to remember your loved one whose existence in your life is already so quickly and sadly fading.

In this phase, many people around you will be embarrassed and upset by your existence and situation and they will either talk to you about it at mind-deadening length or—more often—not only won't talk to you about what you are going through, hoping that'll make it go away, but won't even let you reveal your own feelings. Sometimes when you do reveal your feelings, they'll put them down in various subtle and non-subtle ways, telling you to "grow up," "face facts" or "get on with your life," none of which are very useful to you.

The third phase is the least obvious and the least talked or written about part of widowerhood. Long after the world and those around you have ceased to deal with the problem of your great loss, you're still stuck with it. In many cases, new knowledge about your loved one, or simmering resentments about situations and injustices involving him, suddenly surface and must be dealt with. Bills, letters, and legacy details often take a long time to show up and can be upsetting and infuriating.

In some cases, it is merely that your partner has so defined your life, that now you are completely thrown on your own, you must redefine for yourself who you really are all over again, as you did when you were an adolescent. Remember adolescence? This is a difficult, often harrowing, yet also a potentially wonderful period. This period is crucial to any further life and growth, and to our knowledge this book will contain the first real discussion of it.

Often a great deal depends upon how old you are, i.e., at what stage of your life you are currently in, when your loved one dies. To a healthy thirty year old, the death of even the closest, long term partner will be markedly different than it will be if say you are forty-seven years old, and both of those will be markedly different if you are say sixty-five years old and yourself in poor health. Contained in this book are the stories of men at various places in the life cycle. Less important but still a factor is where you live, how close to family or your gay community.

This book gathers together stories that reflect a diversity of experiences, hoping that men about to lose or who have already lost their partners might find some comfort and validation in hearing what others have been through. I expect that this book will be useful even though it is not set up patently as a "self-help for loss" guide. By having widowers themselves tell their different, richly detailed–very personal–stories, most aspects of the complex process will be illustrated for readers, who then may pick and choose options for coping, and strategies relevant to their own, undoubtedly individual, case.

FELICE'S LIST TO HIS FRIEND

1. His life is not your life. It's his life. His illness is not your illness. It's his illness. His death is not your death. It's his death. You may share in his illness and his death as you shared his life. You are not in control of his life; you have only limited responsibility for it. Keep this in mind at all times.
2. Don't panic. Once you panic you close yourself to opportunity. Keep yourself as calm as possible, especially when he is unable to do so. You will be depended upon to make rational logical choices when he cannot do so. Look into every possibility clearly. Not with hope, not with expectation, but with reality. Who knows, something might ease him, or help him.
3. Ignore people around you. Utilize others' help but rely only on yourself. Do whatever has to be done or whatever you two have agreed to do despite social convention, despite family wishes, despite what "people will say," despite what doctors would like to do "for the future benefit of mankind," despite how you think you'll feel about it later on. Make certain he is not in any pain. Be true to this and you won't regret it afterward.
4. Call me when you need me to repeat this to you.

Felice Picano

Acknowledgments

I wish to thank all of the men who have written chapters for *Gay Widowers*. Without their willingness to share their experiences this book would never been born. I applaud their honesty, vulnerability and openness. In addition to the contributors, there are three individuals who have been essential to the inception, development and completion of this book.

First I wish to thank Raymond Mark Berger, PhD, for his enthusiasm for this project and generosity in offering to solicit Bill Cohen and the people at Haworth/Harrington Park Press about publishing it.

For many years, even before I had the good fortune to meet and become friends with her, Betty Berzon, PhD, has been a constant source of inspiration and support. I firmly believe that she is one of the mothers of contemporary gay and lesbian affirmative psychotherapy and counseling. I will be forever grateful to her for urging me to write about my experiences immediately following my partner's death, and for encouraging me to pursue developing the idea into a book. Her consistent generosity with her time and willingness to read rough drafts and provide insightful, intelligent criticism and suggestions make her an invaluable resource as well as a valued and beloved friend and mentor.

Carl Locke, MSW, has also been exceptionally patient and generous in wading through and editing numerous drafts of my essays in this book. His astute observations and suggestions have been critical to honing the book into its final form.

Introduction

Michael Shernoff

After my partner, Lee, died from his long battle with AIDS, I found that I was drawn to those other gay widowers, men, like myself, who had lost their beloved and were now casting around for some way to make sense of it, some way to figure out how to think of the future as something other than eternal mourning. One man, Jon, whom I had only casually known at the gym, searched me out on the work-out floor to express his condolences, and then we spent half an hour sharing our experiences of being gay widowers–his lover had died from Hepatitis a few years earlier. There was a gentleness in our interactions from that time on, each encounter at the gym or on the street a surprisingly honest moment. I would marvel at how easy it had become to describe how I was adjusting to life without Lee, sharing my inner life, with an acquaintance. I was surprised by how hungry I was for the comfort of this connection and others that similarly were forged in the aftermath of Lee's death. My family, my friends, my therapist and even Lee's family were not enough to hold me through the pain of losing my lover, but those gay widowers who had walked the path before me were my indispensable guides and wise teachers.

Jon was the first of what became an informal network of gay

Michael Shernoff, MSW, is a psychotherapist in private practice in Manhattan and can be reached via e-mail at: mshernoff@aol.com or at his home page: http://members.aol.com/therapysvc.

[Haworth co-indexing entry note]: "Introduction." Shernoff, Michael. Co-published simultaneously in *Journal of Gay & Lesbian Social Services* (The Haworth Press, Inc.) Vol. 7, No. 2, 1997, pp. 1-5; and: *Gay Widowers: Life After the Death of a Partner* (ed: Michael Shernoff) The Haworth Press, Inc., 1997, pp. 1-5; and: *Gay Widowers: Life After the Death of a Partner* (ed: Michael Shernoff) The Harrington Park Press, an imprint of The Haworth Press, Inc., 1997, pp. 1-5. Single or multiple copies of this article are available for a fee from The Haworth Document Delivery Service [1-800-342-9678, 9:00 a.m. - 5:00 p.m. (EST). E-mail address: getinfo@haworth.com].

1

widowers who offered their stories and sympathy to me during that hard first year of being without Lee. As I fumbled through life as a middle-aged, grief-stricken gay man, the gay widowers who made themselves available to me asked me questions and shared practical advice to help me move on in a positive way, without blocking out what the years with Lee had meant to me. We talked about when it might feel right to remove the wedding band, when would it be wise to start dating again, even having sex again, what kind of ongoing relationship, if any, was possible with Lee's family, legal questions about the estate and clearing out his closets.

After a decade of the AIDS epidemic and overwhelming, unspeakable losses in the gay community, I assumed there would be a whole literature about the experience of being a gay widower—from etiquette to self-help. But the only writings I found that spoke from the perspective of being a gay widower were sections in memoirs like Mark Doty's *Heaven's Coast,* some of Paul Monette's superb essays in *Last Watch of the Night,* and his powerfully raging poems *Love Alone: Eighteen Elegies for Rog.* A well-meaning but rather superficial book on *Surviving the Loss of a Loved One to AIDS* was not geared specifically to the surviving partner. It was Monette who once again proved himself to be the contemporary gay bard, poignantly describing how he had survived the process I was just beginning, and I was deeply moved, validated and also terrified. In addition I was eternally grateful to him and his eloquence, vulnerability, and passion. I was desperate for information on what I needed to do to promote the healing I longed for.

I was astounded to find there was not a specific book by or about the process of gay men becoming widowers on the shelves. Thinking that either I had overlooked the book, or perhaps, with all the men in our community whose partners had recently died, they were out of stock, but this was not the case. There was no book for gay widowers. In fact, there were few books written directly for men of any sexual orientation about becoming a widower. Most of the books were written by and for women who had outlived their husband or partner. I determined that I would obtain a book that would speak to me as a man, and a gay man who had lost his partner, one way or another, and so I now find myself editing this anthology, trying to fill in a gap that I, myself, experienced first-hand. My hope is that those souls who find themselves facing the yawning gulf of their grief, and wonder where to turn will be able to use this anthology of wise words from those who have walked the path before them, and will find useful information and soothing reassurance in its pages.

Over the years, I had savored the edited collections compiled by John Preston. I was particularly moved and touched by his anthologies *Hometowns: Gay Men Write About Where They Belong*; *A Member of the Family: Gay Men Write About Their Families*, and *Friends and Lovers: Gay Men Write About the Families They Create*. Each provides a window into a variety of different aspects of gay mens' lives. They are not merely personal testimonies (even if they were, they would be invaluable records of lives lived), but each is in fact an exhilarating social history. Preston's gift to us and to the writers in his books is that he provided vehicles for so many voices to be heard. These works have insured that any gay person, but certainly young gay men, can find reflections of themselves in print, an invaluable contribution at a time when we are still lacking positive mirroring in the media. *Gay Widowers* is modeled on the anthologies Preston so lovingly edited, and it is my belief that it is also a stunning social history, documenting what it means to lose a partner and begin life anew as a gay man in the 1990s. In compiling these essays, I invited the contributors to write something that they themselves would have wanted to read when they were in the midst of adapting to their new condition as widowers, suggesting they try to describe both the pain of this transition as well as what was helpful to them. I urged them to be as personal as possible, and regard the writing as both therapeutic and healing, as well as a gift they were offering to our community.

It's important for this book to transcend the AIDS epidemic. The epidemic has defined our community for so long that many people forget that gay men have always, and continue to die from causes other than AIDS. At the same time, the experience of men who have lost a partner to AIDS is very much part of this book, with a particular emphasis on how the surviving partner can cope, and eventually thrive again in a vastly changed world. Many of the essays describe surviving a partner's death from AIDS, but there are also stories by men whose partners died suddenly of natural causes and other illnesses.

George Seabold begins the collection with a harrowing tale of how mourning the death of his long time lover was complicated by his not being publicly identified as a gay man. This story that takes place decades before the onset of AIDS is a window into a time in the not so distant past that remains the reality even today for who knows how many thousands of people who do not have the privilege or ability to publicly declare themselves as gay people and avail themselves of a community and support. Eric Gutierrez's interview with Don Bachardy describes how Bachardy transformed himself after the death of his partner of several decades, Christopher Isherwood. In his interview with Eric Gutierrez, Bachardy describes how he experienced a complete role reversal in the relationship that followed the one he cherished with Christopher. It is also fitting that Paul Monette's partner, Winston Wilde, tells part of his story of recreating himself from Mrs. Paul Monette to Mr. Winston Wilde. In talking with Winston during the preparation of this book, he told me that Paul had told him "Winnie, tell people our story, tell them how we loved each other in the midst of this plague." I believe that Paul would have been pleased to have the story of how the love he and Winston shared fueled Winston's evolution following his death. After all, Paul was one of the best loved and most well respected authors of "our tribe," as he so often referred to gay people in his writings. There are essays by and about relationships with well known and prominent gay men as well as by and about relationships with ordinary men, all of whom share the dubious distinction of having loved greatly and lost the person they adored.

This book contains a widely diverse cross section of our community. Thus, men of different ages and racial, ethnic, religious, geographic and economic backgrounds are all included. My hope is that if your lover is currently dying, this book will provide you with some hope for a meaningful life after he has gone, while beginning to prepare you for the realities of just how difficult a transition awaits you. If you are a recent or even a not-so-recent widower, I expect that you will find some of your experiences reflected in the stories, and discover an additional source of comfort in recognizing some of what you are currently going through, or have gone through. If, by some chance, you are not gay and are reading this book, I sincerely hope that you will come to understand the universality of the human experience as told by the men who have shared their experiences in the following pages. If you are a member of one of the helping professions my hope is that the stories told in the following pages will help you in your work with all clients, but specifically gay men who are about to or who have already become widowers. I hope that you will find this book to be a useful and friendly companion as you navigate these uncharted waters.

Surviving a Partner's Death
Deeply in the Closet

George Seabold

Today, as I write this essay, I am sixty-six years old, and have been a widower for eighteen years. My lover Wes and I had known each other for twenty years and had lived together as lovers for over fifteen years. Wes and I both worked for the U.S. government in the aerospace industry and each had top secret security clearances. This was not an easy feat to carry off in those post-McCarthy days. We were two gay men, lovers, who lived together who needed to maintain the illusion of heterosexuality in order to keep our clearances, and our incomes. During the 1960s, in the aerospace industry, the ability to maintain a security clearance was mandatory as prerequisite for employment. No clearance–no job. Period!

One very important section of the application for clearance were questions regarding the applicant's personal lifestyle, which implied sexual preference. The degree of clearance determined how thoroughly the government decided to investigate. Confidential clearance wasn't too bad. But secret, top secret or above resulted in background checks and interviews with every one of your personal references, neighbors, landlords, other tenants, and everybody from the friendly grocer to the locker room attendant at the local athletic

George Seabold is a retired logistics engineer formerly with the United States aerospace industry currently living in Oxnard, CA.

[Haworth co-indexing entry note]: "Surviving a Partner's Death Deeply in the Closet." Seabold, George. Co-published simultaneously in *Journal of Gay & Lesbian Social Services* (The Haworth Press, Inc.) Vol. 7, No. 2, 1997, pp. 7-14; and: *Gay Widowers: Life After the Death of a Partner* (ed: Michael Shernoff) The Haworth Press, Inc., 1997, pp. 7-14; and: *Gay Widowers: Life After the Death of a Partner* (ed: Michael Shernoff) The Harrington Park Press, an imprint of The Haworth Press, Inc., 1997, pp. 7-14. Single or multiple copies of this article are available for a fee from The Haworth Document Delivery Service [1-800-342-9678, 9:00 a.m. - 5:00 p.m. (EST). E-mail address: getinfo@haworth.com].

club. Despite the intensity of the scrutiny, both Wes and I managed to maintain top secret clearances, even after he became ill, and for me after his death. Wes and I were deeply in the closet and as you will hear, this was not without a cost to us emotionally, socially and spiritually!

Though we never explicitly discussed being gay or being lovers with our families, during our years together Wes, his mother and maiden aunt had been accepted as members of my family, and similarly I was accepted as another son by his mother. Our collective families would celebrate birthdays, holidays and all special occasions together as one large extended family. Thus, without pretending or hiding the nature of our very special and intimate relationship, we received support from our families and somehow were able to maintain our clearances and livelihood at the same time.

We met while employed at the same company, and both worked there until he had to retire due to the debilitating effects of the malignant brain tumor that ultimately killed him. We did attempt to appear to everyone at work as just good friends and roommates. This facade may not have fooled anyone, but was the best we could do during those difficult years prior to the Clinton administration's change in policy regarding being gay as a reason for a person to be denied a security clearance, even at the highest level. The subject of our lifestyle was never openly discussed at work or with either of our families, and yet we lived our lives as a committed male couple.

We both lived and worked in the San Fernando Valley. Our home was within five miles of where we worked. Outside of work we were inseparable. Behind our closed doors, we felt safe and carried on as any other pair of lovers would. Publicly together we did all the household activities that any couple does, grocery shopping, dropping off and picking up the dry cleaning, and having our cars serviced. But to all appearances we were two men who just lived together. But on the very rare occasion that we did go into one of the gay establishments we lived in fear that someone from work would see us and it would result in losing our clearances and our jobs. The only two places we felt comfortable to be ourselves as a male couple was when we either vacationed on Maui in a motor home we rented, or at the only gay resort that existed at that time in Palm Springs, as far away from prying eyes as we could easily go.

We went about living our lives and tried not to worry too much about being exposed as gay, losing our security clearances or being fired. Perhaps we were naive, but less than ten years after the McCarthy anti-gay pogroms no one was talking about homosexuals so we felt relatively safe. We just never discussed being gay with anyone at work or at our church where we both sang in the choir. We did not know any other gay people or have any other gay friends. We were completely isolated from the gay community and as a result we were totally dependent upon each other. All of our friends were heterosexual and may have assumed that we were gay, but no one ever broached this subject with either of us. Even though we were living a constricted life, we were extremely happy and did not think that things could ever be different. This reality set the stage for how I dealt with Wes's illness and ultimate death.

In 1977, after several months of experiencing hideous headaches, Wes was diagnosed as having a cancerous brain tumor. About this time my mother was admitted to a convalescent hospital because my seventy-six year old father could no longer take care of her at home. Thus, began the single most stressful period of my life. Once the brain tumor was removed Wes began a debilitating round of chemotherapy and radiation beginning his fatal decline. About a year before he died, it began to dawn on me that he was in fact going to die and that I was going to lose him. Even with this growing recognition of the inevitability of his death I never thought about what my life would be like after Wes died, and never planned for this eventuality.

As his condition worsened, Wes could no longer drive and needed someone to take him to various medical appointments. As his partner, I took time off from work to drive him to medical appointments. Thank goodness that my boss knew and liked Wes and permitted me to be flexible in my work times. I was never recognized as Wes's partner by any of the medical offices we dealt with even though I was handling all of his finances and insurance forms. Though I was a devoted mate, no one ever mentioned anything to either Wes or me about what we were going through. There was literally no support for us as individuals and certainly none for us as a couple. Perhaps support would have been available to us had we been open about the nature of our relationship, but we were too concerned about maintaining our ability to make a living to even dream of confiding in anyone, not even the pastor of our church. The truth was that even had support been available to us, we did not know how to identify potentially sympathetic individuals or agencies that might have been helpful to us as a couple or to me later on as a grieving widower.

My mother died in October, 1978 at about the same time that Wes was told he only had thirty to sixty days to live. This news prompted him to tell his mother and aunt about his condition and he decided he wanted us to take his eighty-three year old mother and his seventy-three year old aunt to Maui. He was wheel chair bound by this time, but off we went to "the closest thing to paradise he had found on earth." Wes died six days after we arrived in Hawaii, and I immediately went into an "automatic pilot" way of sleepwalking through the remaining days of that trip as I continued to play tour guide to Wes's mother and aunt. Wes had told his mother that he wanted to be cremated and have his ashes scattered in Maui. Luckily she complied with his wishes, because I had no legal authority to act on behalf of my own lover. I had kept up a facade of having a stiff upper lip during the time in Hawaii and on the seemingly endless flight home for his mother's sake. But once I arrived home and entered our apartment without Wes for the first time in fifteen years, I slumped to the floor just inside the front door and at long last just fell apart. The next few days are still, to this day, a complete blank, which most likely was the result of my making regular and extended visits to our well stocked bar.

With Wes gone, I fell into a deep funk. I had nobody to talk to as all of my friends were straight and did not realize the extent of my loss or the depth of my feelings. I returned to work in a haze and hardly received any acknowledgment of Wes's death there. I went even deeper into the closet and started drinking regularly. Many people describe losing themselves in work following the death of a spouse. For me, work offered no respite from my grief. Wes and I had not only worked for the same company, but by the time he got sick he was working with me, literally sitting at the next desk. So throughout my work day, each glance at Wes's vacant desk was a terribly painful and visceral reminder of the loss of my beloved.

Wes and I had both sung in the church choir and made friends with straight people in the choir. But during the year that Wes was sick we pulled away from most other people and activities and thus after his death there was not anyone around for me. I did not reach out to the hetero people we had been friends with previously. I stopped attending church services and really withdrew into myself. Since the pastor of our church had never reached out to us during Wes's illness, I did not seek him out after Wes's death. As a couple we had not made any close friends, and as a result I was totally on my own after his death.

Prior to Wes's death I was only a social drinker. Our normal routine had been to have a couple of drinks together before dinner. After he died, each evening when I returned home to our apartment I would still have those initial couple of drinks, but I did not stop with a couple. I had been the one who prepared our meals, and Wes would clean up. After he died I lost all interest in cooking for myself and hardly ate. Thus the amount of alcohol I consumed was having a greater effect on me due to my not having eaten. Each night I would either drink until I stumbled to bed, or passed out in the living room. For the first eight to twelve months following Wes's death I completely isolated myself from the rest of the world socially except for an occasional foray to one of the local bath houses.

I worked, came home, drank and never visited a straight or gay bar. Once Wes was gone, I tried to continue on with my life and do by myself the things we used to enjoy together. But alone it just wasn't the same, so my isolation worsened. Soon I became a regular at the local bath house seeking distraction from my pain, loneliness and despair in sexual escapades. Within six months of becoming a widower I met someone at the baths who I naively felt could fill the void created by Wes's death. Of course that was foolish, and I should not have considered starting another relationship so soon. But I was desperately lonely after having lived so closely and inti-mately with Wes for so long, I confused my needs for some human interaction and affection with something deeper and more pro-found.

My drinking increased which did not help my budding relation-ship with Adolph. I left my job with the aerospace company and became a consultant for the U.S. Air Force. The requirement for the security clearance remained the same, but the contact with the government was even more direct. My friend moved into my apartment. We lived together, slept together, partied together, and even eventually bought a house together. Yet something was definitely missing. I was looking for Wes but didn't know at that time that I could never find him again. At this time I began psychotherapy and began to learn that part of my current distress was that I had never taken the time to actively mourn either Wes or my mother. At the time I had no idea what this meant. How do you make yourself grieve on cue?

This partnership lasted for six years until Adolph married a Filipina woman he was friends with at work whose visa was about to expire. This was entirely a marriage of convenience in order for her to remain in the United States, but unbeknownst to me they had occasionally had sex when I was out of town. Adolph moved in with her and I bought out his half of our house when she became pregnant. Adolph asked me to be the godfather of his second child, a son. Thus once again I was alone, suffering a major loss without anyone to confide in since I had stopped seeing my therapist. Just like Wes and I had done, Adolph and I had never made friends with any other gay people. With my parents dead, my life was totally bound up in work and my relationship with my lover. Until there was a crisis I didn't know that I needed people besides my lover in my life. Even then, I hadn't the vaguest idea of how to meet people and become close to them.

Soon after Adolph moved in with his wife, my drinking really became a problem. By the time I was working for the Air Force as a consultant I would attend business meetings and forget what I had agreed to do and the schedule I had committed myself to. I was consumed with feeling sorry for myself and just did not know what to do in order to help myself feel better as there was literally no one else in my life. I was lonely as hell and, never having been connected to other gay people, had no idea of how to begin to end the isolation. Shortly after the birth of my godson, returning from a party, I was stopped by the highway patrol on the freeway for driving under the influence. My drinking had finally caught up with me and I spent the night in jail.

Even before being arrested for drunk driving I had wanted to stop drinking but did not know how. After the arrest I called a straight friend who I had known for over thirty years who had been sober for more than ten years. I reasoned that since he had taught me how to drink, he could now help me stop. I began to attend AA meetings that were all straight but never shared that I was gay or had lost anyone more important to me than a close friend. For six to eight months after first beginning to attend AA, I'd go to the meetings, then stop at a liquor store on my way home and continue to drink.

I tried going to a few local gay AA meetings, but I never spoke at them, rationalizing my silence as being due to the fact that I didn't know anyone at these meetings. I quickly stopped going to the gay meetings convincing myself that the reason I stopped was because I was afraid that someone from work would see me, and jeopardize my job. Now, looking back, in hind sight, I realize that the only way I ever could have begun to meet any of the sober gay folks would have been by doing precisely what I was most afraid of, opening my mouth, talking about who I was, what I was going through and what I was feeling. This was something I felt completely ill equipped to do. I was consumed by fears, and lacked any understanding of what I now know is homophobia and how it crippled me for most of my life. Today I am clear that for more than two decades it was easier to camouflage all of my fears as only having to do with the security clearance issue and job security than it would have been to struggle with creating a dignified and full life for myself and my lover. The reality was that for far too many years I had no idea that any gay man could live a life not ruled by fears nor preoccupied with hiding what he was and who he loved.

I was finally motivated to stop drinking one night when I was at a meeting where a celebrity, who I had admired on the stage and in movies received a cake celebrating the anniversary of his ninth year sober. There and then I made up my mind that if he could give up drinking, so could I, and I have been sober since then for the past nine years. Only when I became sober was I finally able to begin to fully experience the full range of my pain about the death of Wes and how Adolph's leaving exacerbated all of the feelings I had been keeping bottled up. Newly sober I was consumed with feeling sorry for myself. I had no idea why this was all happening to me. I was bewildered and felt like I was walking around in a haze, only now I was not either drunk or hung over. Most of all I was terribly lonely and unbelievably sad.

Clinton's signing the proclamation that being gay was no longer a reason to be denied any level of security clearance freed me up to begin to socialize in gay environments openly and unafraid. Two years before I retired I joined the Gay Men's Chorus of Los Angeles, but would absent myself from any photos or television appearances because I was not at that time yet comfortable being completely out as gay. I finally retired in 1995 and immediately afterwards began to fully come out as a gay man. I no longer hide who I am or watch what I say.

Writing this essay has clarified for me that my mourning of Wes, even though he died 18 years ago, is still not over. I continue to miss him terribly and long for the life I had hoped we would have had together. For the past year and a half I have been dating a wonderfully loving man who, of course, knows all about Wes. Leo and I are committed to each other, and we live without any pretense about the nature of our relationship. But I feel differently about Leo than I did about Wes. Wes was my first and greatest love. I finally have a life as an openly gay man with gay friends, who is able to comfortably socialize in gay milieus. I'm enjoying my life in emotionally open and uninhibited ways I had never dreamed were possible. I never take this freedom for granted. I only wish that Wes was around so we could have shared this transition and new found freedom; marveling and basking together at arriving at a place where fears no longer rule our lives.

Do You Have a Partner?

Michael Shernoff

Being in grief, it turns out, is not unlike being in love. In both states,
the imagination's entirely occupied with one person. The beloved dwells
at the heart of the world, and becomes a Rome: the roads of feeling all
lead to him, all proceed from him. Everything that touches us seems to relate back to that center;
there is no other emotional life, no place outside the universe of
feeling centered on its pivotal figure. And in grief, as in love, we're porous, permeable. There
is something contagious about this openness. Other people sense
it and respond to us differently, since our guardedness seems to invite them in.

–Mark Doty, *Heaven's Coast*

Lee died at home, in our bed, and at first I was relieved that he was not suffering any longer, but then, immediately, I felt more lonely than I had ever remembered being, as well as terrified by what seemed like the overwhelming burden of living without my adored friend, partner and soul mate. Near the end of Lee's life, there were moments I found myself thinking that it would be better for both of us if he were just to die already. This is something I have often heard expressed by friends, lovers or family members of a terminally ill individual who is suffering greatly. Sometimes this comes out of the caretaker's feeling that he or she has reached his or her limits, but often it is a compassionate response to not wanting a loved one to go on in the manner they have been.

Michael Shernoff, MSW, is a psychotherapist in private practice in Manhattan and can be reached vie e-mail at: mshernoff@aol.com or at his home page: http://members.aol.com/therapysvc.

[Haworth co-indexing entry note]: "Do You Have a Partner?" Shernoff, Michael. Co-published simultaneously in *Journal of Gay & Lesbian Social Services* (The Haworth Press, Inc.) Vol. 7, No. 2, 1997, pp. 15-28; and: *Gay Widowers: Life After the Death of a Partner* (ed: Michael Shernoff) The Haworth Press, Inc., 1997, pp. 15-28; and: *Gay Widowers: Life After the Death of a Partner* (ed: Michael Shernoff) The Harrington Park Press, an imprint of The Haworth Press, Inc., 1997, pp. 15-28. Single or multiple copies of this article are available for a fee from The Haworth Document Delivery Service [1-800-342-9678, 9:00 a.m. - 5:00 p.m. (EST). E-mail address: getinfo@haworth.com].

15

In his final months, Lee openly spoke of being ready to die. His quality of life had enormously diminished since he couldn't read any more, or even follow a mindless television show, making his days torturously long and interminable. Though both of my parents, my oldest brother, best friends, numerous other close friends, and over one hundred men whom I had seen as psychotherapy patients had all died, I had never before been present at the actual moment someone made the transition out of life. It was startling in its suddenness. One moment this man was lying in our bed struggling for breath and the next he was silent and calm, having left the world we shared. One moment I was a devoted partner, caring for my beloved mate, and the next I was a widower. Witnessing Lee's death was humbling and precious, as was knowing that he trusted me to follow his wishes exactly during this critical period when he couldn't be in control for himself. I realized that the previous 10 years of counseling people with AIDS and their loved ones had all been preparation for being with and helping Lee throughout this final phase of his life in addition to helping me cope with my own grieving.

When I called the funeral home, the man I spoke to asked me when I wanted them to pick up the body. Since about a dozen of our friends were at the apartment at this point, I told him I'd call back when I was ready for them to come to take Lee away. After all of our friends except one had left, I called and asked the undertakers to come in half an hour. I climbed back into bed with Lee, held him and told him how glad I was that he no longer looked frightened or tormented. Most difficult was when, with tears streaming down my face, I removed the wedding band I had given him. This was the moment when his death and what it would mean for my future life became real to me. I literally had forgotten to breathe while I was taking off his ring. Clutching his wedding band, I watched the man I loved, and had shared every aspect of my life with for the previous three short years, being wheeled out of our apartment, inside a black vinyl body bag. As he disappeared into the elevator I broke down and collapsed into my friend Ed's arms.

Earlier, two friends had asked if I wanted someone to spend the night. Thanking them, I declined their sweet offer. I knew I needed to be alone and begin to experience being in the home Lee and I had joyously shared without him. One of our friends inquired about whether I felt it would be too morbid to sleep in the bed where Lee died. That had never occurred to me, but did create a nervousness about sleeping in our bed. Yet, burrowing under the covers, that first night as well as on numerous subsequent nights, I thought of our bed as a sacred site, the place where we spent hours making love, cuddling and sleeping. What a logical extension of all our shared intimacy that he would die there as well.

The day after Lee died, I went to the funeral home to arrange for the cremation and sending his ashes to his parents in Georgia. While there, I told the funeral director I wanted to see Lee. We had our final good bye in a viewing room at Redden's Funeral Parlor, two blocks from where we lived and where he had died. He was on a stretcher, still within the black vinyl body bag in which he had been brought out of our apartment. Someone had unzipped and folded down the top of the bag over his shoulders, exposing his head, neck and the top of his chest, startling white in contrast to the dark body bag. I was shocked by just how cold and lifeless his skin and lips were as I stroked them crying, knowing that this would be the last time I ever saw this beautiful man who had challenged me to love and create a shared life. I don't remember everything I said or felt that morning. I do remember telling him that I would never forget him, and that if I ever fell in love again it would largely be because of all I learned from him and our time together. I remember trying to memorize each detail of how he looked, lying there looking so relaxed and peaceful, and how it felt to touch him and graze his now nonresponsive lips with mine.

I wanted to freeze that moment as if he hadn't already left me, venturing on his final journey alone. Prior to going in to see Lee, I called several friends to inquire whether they wanted to join me at the funeral home. None of them was at home, so I took that to be a sign that this was meant to be our time alone together. Looking down at Lee before I left him for the last time, I remember breathing very deeply and thinking what an unbridgeable distance already separated us. How bizarre it was feeling so acutely alone and simultaneously so connected to someone no longer living.

Even knowing that Lee's death was inevitable had not prepared me for just how painful and difficult the transition was to being a widower. I was completely caught off guard the day after Lee died.

It was as if I was living under a perpetual gray cloud for weeks after Lee died. How dare the world not mirror my emotional state! How dare the world continue to function normally as if there wasn't now this enormous gaping hole where previously there had been a life!

Lee's death affected every facet of my life, and even impacted upon my functioning as a psychotherapist. His obituary appeared in *The New York Times*, so the fact of his death and my being listed as his "adoring partner" was public. Half of my clients sent me condolence cards or notes and expressed sympathy on my loss. Suddenly, people who hadn't known anything or very much about my personal life, knew a very important detail that intimately affected me. When clients asked how I was doing, I honestly told them how difficult I was finding adjusting to life without Lee.

Some clients talked about wanting to take care of me out of a desire to repay my helpfulness over the years. Whenever I heard this, I told the person how much it meant to hear them express such caring for me and value for the work we had been doing. But I told them that the best gift they could give me was to work hard during our sessions together. I explained that my pain and grieving would be with me almost constantly, but one of the very few times I was not consumed with thoughts and feelings about Lee was when I was concentrating on and listening carefully to a client. Most clients told me that they were grateful that I had been open with them in sharing a bit of what I was going through instead of retreating behind the facade of professional psychotherapist. In the months that followed, numerous clients said that hearing me acknowledge my pain so openly made it easier for them to feel safe in revealing painful and vulnerable issues that they might have shied away from disclosing had they not experienced me as a real person with real problems of his own. Two patients told me that observing me working and functioning well professionally in the midst of my grief served as a role model for them to face extremely painful situations with the confidence that they would be able to survive what they had previously feared would be overwhelming circumstances.

Another way that Lee's death has affected my work is that I am constantly examining any assumptions I may have about what empathizing with or understanding a client's pain actually consists of. I thought that by having counseled many men whose partners had

died, that I would know what to expect in terms of my own grieving. I couldn't have been more mistaken. Thus I realize that in order
to truly connect with my clients, I now make more of an effort to
ask them to explain what they are feeling in greater detail, insuring
that I hear from them their experiences in tremendous detail. Of
course, I always had done this to some extent prior to Lee's death;
now, I do it more assiduously, without ever assuming that I can
understand how a person is feeling unless they elaborate.

In addition, I judiciously share more personal information with
certain clients. This occurs with clients who I have been seeing for
several years and who are really struggling with something uncomfortable or painful. I have on occasion said things to clients who
know about Lee's death, "Do you think I want to hurt as bad as I
am? It's just that I have no choice other than to acknowledge those
feelings and continue on while having them." In another instance I
told a man who was struggling with dating, "I know exactly how
you feel as someone who is also going through the process of trying
to meet people." Clients report back to me that these comments
have been useful in reminding them that my life isn't perfect and
without struggles.

Immediately after Lee died, I went on automatic pilot, taking
care of all of the myriad details of his estate. Walking around, I felt
like one of those old hard-hat deep-sea divers one sees in films
plodding along the ocean bottom in lead boots. Our apartment
seemed enormous and I purchased some new living room furniture
and carpets. I also planned several trips. We were supposed to go to
Belize over Thanksgiving, but Lee's deterioration forced us to cancel that trip. Scuba diving has always been one of my greatest
escapes, so after Lee died I booked myself into the dive resort in
Belize where we had planned to stay. That was three weeks after
Lee's death, and I was hoping to dive myself silly in an effort to
distract myself from my pain and generally feeling so pessimistic
and overwhelmed.

The trip was a disaster insofar as I was the only guest at the resort
on a small atoll, a ninety minute boat ride from Belize City. In
between diving there was no one to talk with. It seemed painfully
romantic and in hindsight it was a major error in judgment to go
somewhere where I had no access to a phone and so could not be in

close contact with my friends. I cried the entire plane ride down remembering Lee's final hours, and finally called two friends from the plane just to talk and seek consolation. After four days of wonderful diving and interminably long nights spent sitting on the dock talking to Lee and crying as I relived each aspect of his final illness, I left three days early and returned home feeling anything but refreshed or distracted from my inconsolable feelings.

As a therapist who had counseled more than 50 men whose partners had died, I thought I would be prepared for the progression of my mourning. What hubris!! I couldn't have been more wrong. I was knocked flat on my ass by the intensity of all that I felt in the weeks and months following Lee's death. All I could do was to constantly remind myself that I was powerless over my mourning. My only choice seemed to be to surrender to the experience and ride the waves of feelings that, even a year after his death, threatened to overwhelm me. I knew this was how I would get through this particular phase of my grieving in the healthiest way. From observing friends and clients who had lost a partner, I also knew that these feelings would diminish over time, and that eventually I would feel better.

After Lee's death, I developed a new form of "Gay-dar," which was an ability to ferret out and meet other gay widowers. Wherever I went, I found myself invariably engaged in a conversation with someone else whose partner had died. There is always an immediate intimacy and gentleness in these connections that is poignant for both of us and immeasurably comforting. Two months after Lee's death, while attending a memorial dinner party for a friend, I was introduced to Dennis, whose partner, Ian, had died 14 months earlier. We spent hours sharing the stories of what we had each been through, laughing at similarities and feeling close as only two people who have shared similar traumatic experiences can. We exchanged phone numbers and I called him the next day to make plans to have dinner that weekend. Though I knew I found him terribly attractive, at that point I hadn't even begun to think about dating. Our talks about what each of us had gone through in caring for our sick partners, and what life was like afterwards created an immediate bond that I only felt with other men who had been through what I was now living.

The first night that Dennis and I made love and he slept over was the very first time I ever dreamed about Lee. In my dream, he was not angry, nor judgmental, just very present. I told this to Dennis over breakfast the following morning. After he inquired about whether I was alright with our having had sex, he laughed and asked how I felt about that dream. I remember telling him that it was unsettling, but not disturbing. Dennis and I began to see each other, initially both of us totally clear about neither wanting nor being ready for another serious relationship. Yet as we became friends, spending time together going to the theater, dance recitals, dinners and parties and sleeping together regularly, it was clear that we had begun to date. As it became apparent to the two of us that a variety of strong feelings and attachments were forming, Dennis and I each expressed caution, wonder and extreme nervousness.

The first extremely difficult moment in dating Dennis occurred the evening of my first birthday following Lee's death. I had not looked forward to that day, as celebrations were something Lee and I always took very seriously, and assiduously observed. Thus I approached my birthday with more than a small dose of dread. Dennis was very sweet and asked if he could take me out to dinner. Part of me just wanted to pretend that there was nothing special about that particular day. I felt both resentful and flattered that Dennis wanted to do something special for my birthday. I resented it because he wasn't Lee, and I'd rather have been pouting and feeling sorry for myself alone at home. The healthier and more rational part of me was thoroughly enjoying what seemed to be a courtship ritual.

When Dennis left the message at my office to meet him at The Gotham Bar and Grill on East 12th Street, my heart sank. This was the same restaurant where Lee had taken me the previous year to celebrate my birthday, and I had not been back since. I wrestled with whether or not to call Dennis and ask if we could go to another restaurant and explain why. Ultimately, I decided that this was merely the first of innumerable experiences I would face in the weeks and months ahead of finding myself returning to places for the first time without Lee. It was with heaviness and ambivalence that I walked to the restaurant. As I came closer, my pace slowed down, as if I could postpone or avoid going in and feeling melancholy and preoccupied. I even debated whether or not it was fair to Dennis to even tell him what was going on for me. I knew that if I didn't share all of this with Dennis there was no possible way that either of us could feel close and connected that evening. After kissing each other "hello" and my giving him a longer hug than usual in a public place, I told him that this was where Lee and I had celebrated my birthday last year. With his usual sensitivity, he asked me if I'd rather go somewhere else. That was all it took for me to describe what I was feeling to his warm and compassionate nods and gentle touches throughout dinner. We laughed at the irony that of all the restaurants in Manhattan, he had chosen this one, and took it as a sign that I was strong enough to continue my grieving and healing in unexpected ways and places.

A similar ironic coincidence occurred three months later when we decided to rent a room in a house on Fire Island for the Fourth of July weekend. A sign posted on the bulletin board of my gym advertised that rooms were available to sublet in a pool house in The Pines. When I spoke to the man who was seeking to rent his room and asked where the house was, he gave me the address of the house that I had rented for four years. This was the same house that Lee and I had spent our first summer as a couple. What was even more startling was that Dennis and I would be renting the very same room that Lee and I occupied three years earlier! I told the man what my hesitations were about renting the room, and told him I'd get back to him soon.

Dennis said that if I didn't want to rent that place he would of course understand, and we'd find another. After giving it some thought and really laughing at the unlikeliness of such a chance occurrence happening, I thought that it might be very healing to go back to a place where Lee and I had been very happy. If I believed in angels or an afterlife, I would swear that this was both a sign from Lee that I needed to move ahead, as well as his way of playing a practical joke on me. In the introduction to the *Tevye Stories*, Sholom Alechim writes: "Coincidences are not coincidences after all, but only the means by which a series of seemingly unrelated events get brought into focus." This certainly seemed to apply to my life.

One evening right before what would have been Lee's 33rd birthday, his parents called to thank me for sending them a large photo collage I put together for his memorial service. During that conversation, his father asked me if I met anyone yet. For the first time since meeting Dennis, I felt embarrassed to admit that I had begun to date. I was afraid that they were going to judge me and feel that it was too soon after the death of their son for me to be seeing another man. After what felt like an awkwardly long silence, I responded honestly that I had begun seeing someone a few months previously, another widower who was kind, fun and sensitive. Without a moment's hesitation Lee's dad exuberantly said that he was so pleased and happy for me and that he was certain that Lee would have wanted that as well. I became all choked up and weepy as I felt his genuine, loving concern for my well-being. As I spoke with Lee's mother about how difficult the coming weeks were going to be around his birthday and the anniversary of his death, we both broke down and shared our pain and tears across the miles.

In the fourth month of dating, Dennis told me that he felt that he was ready to settle down again, and he was falling in love with me. Initially, I resisted making a commitment to him. After a few more weeks of thinking back on how my time with Lee had been the happiest period of my life, and that this sweet, kind, sexy man was offering me the opportunity to partner up again, I happily agreed that I wouldn't see any other men. All was well with us, and we spent a very happy three months until I realized that I had begun to resent Dennis precisely because he wasn't Lee. Somehow, I had just substituted Dennis for Lee. My awareness of this corresponded with the approaching first anniversary of Lee's death, and I stopped seeing Dennis.

After the relationship with Dennis ended, I was thrust back into the same intensity of feelings I had immediately after Lee's death. I missed Dennis some, but missed Lee terribly. While I don't think it was a mistake to have begun dating, especially someone as sensitive and empathic as Dennis, in hindsight I realize I erred by allowing the relationship to become as serious as it did so quickly. Lee and I hadn't been sexual in over a year because of his illness. I was starved for the kind of contact that only a truly intimate sexual and affectionate experience can provide. The sharing that Dennis and I did about Ian and Lee provided a foundation for closeness that fueled our physical passion.

While still missing Lee, dating Dennis provided me with companionship, friendship and a budding romance. What I didn't realize was that it also distracted me from my feelings about Lee and interrupted my mourning. After not having compared Dennis and Lee for months I began to do so. Unfortunately, Dennis came up short. I knew this wasn't fair, yet I couldn't help myself from making those comparisons. As I became increasingly depressed and withdrawn from Dennis, he urged me to talk to him about what I was feeling, and even suggested that I was having an understandable reaction to the approaching anniversary of Lee's death. As much as I might have wanted to, I couldn't reach out to him and thus began a cycle of his shutting down to me in response to my withdrawing from him. My inability to talk with Dennis about what I was feeling for the first time in our relationship was the largest contributing factor to our breaking up.

By telling this story I am not suggesting that any specific amount of time has to pass before a person is ready to date again, or even to get seriously involved following the death of his partner. Unknown to me, I had ceased to actively grieve Lee as I became increasingly involved with Dennis. If I had been more aware of this, I would have resisted committing to Dennis, and simply have continued to date him and see how the relationship evolved. When I first met Dennis, I still thought of myself as a married man. Albeit, someone who was married to a partner now dead, but still married none the less. In hindsight being with Dennis I just slipped back into being actively married again, loving the role and feeling comfortable with it. I even heard myself sometimes calling Dennis "Lee." It was as if I was somehow keeping Lee alive instead of letting him go, which could only happen through mourning. I was in love with being married, but was I in love with Dennis? It was too hard to separate everything out and answer that honestly. As a result of my shutting down and withdrawing emotionally from Dennis, we stopped seeing each other two weeks before the anniversary of Lee's death. Though I was not happy that Dennis was very hurt, and enraged at me, all I could feel about not seeing him any longer was relief.

Immediately after Lee died, I felt as if part of my soul and very essence had been amputated. I doubted that I would ever again feel happy, or even ever again experience the absence of sadness. Gradually, the chronicity of my sadness began to reduce, and two months after Lee's death, I found myself even beginning to occasionally enjoy things again. Thus, I was totally caught off guard about nine months after Lee died by a resurgence of grieving as the constant but gentle waves of mourning, grief and sadness began building into an emotional hurricane that threatened to totally disrupt my equilibrium as well as my normal life. Several times, people told me that I was finally allowing all of the feelings to emerge. I became furious that I was feeling all of these things, and enraged that Lee had died, necessitating my going through all of this emotional turmoil.

Ten months after my partner Lee died, while waiting to cross the street on the corner of Greenwich and Eighth Avenues, out of the corner of my eye I noticed a man with the exact same shade of red hair that Lee had. As I turned to look at him I realized that he was the same body size and shape as Lee had been when he was healthy. Suddenly, what had merely been a growing sense of getting choked up burst out of me in racking sobs. I forgot about the errand I had been about to do, rushed back to my office crying and feeling thoroughly shaken and dazed by how abruptly I had become so vulnerable and fragile. This was indicative of how the period approaching the first anniversary of Lee's death surprised me with a new onslaught of sadness and depression. Even activities that I enjoyed couldn't put a dent in my new mental condition, characterized by a total absence of and incapacity for happiness.

The weeks leading up to the first anniversary of Lee's death found me thrust back to the first days after his death when my entire being was consumed with missing Lee. I began to talk to him (though he never answered). I started to overeat, especially sweets, and couldn't bring myself to exercise. After years of not having bitten my nails, I resumed that nervous habit in addition to picking at my cuticles until they were bloody. On the first anniversary of our learning that he had central nervous system lymphoma, I began to remember in graphic detail the events of the previous year. Each day would bring new and painful memories. Normally, I bound out of bed and either go to the gym after doing a half hour on the Nordic

Track or to the office for an 8 a.m. client. Getting going in the morning was increasingly difficult and I slept more, feeling as if I was drugged. I was chronically sad and quite depressed. I became preoccupied with thoughts about the inevitability of my becoming symptomatic with AIDS and my own death, and even wrestled with whether or not to go on antidepressants. The only people I found comfort in talking to were my therapist and either very old friends or other men whose partners had died.

My desire to have sex diminished, and yet I was simultaneously consumed with wild sexual fantasies about every attractive man I saw, though I didn't feel as if I had the energy to do anything about those fantasies. After years of therapy, I knew that whenever this occurred, it was a strong indication that I really wanted to avoid and run away from profoundly uncomfortable feelings. The only things I really looked forward to were work and losing myself in writing. I felt lost, adrift and generally in a dazed state, similar to how I felt in the weeks immediately following Lee's death. As the anniversary of his death approached, I found myself returning to memories of our final weeks together and often felt emotionally more attached to the previous year, with Lee, than connected to the present.

Looking for some form of community service to do on Thanksgiving day, a year after Lee's death, I called God's Love We Deliver, an agency that delivers hot meals to home-bound people with AIDS. I reached a lovely woman, Vivian, who was glad to sign me up as a volunteer delivery person. After gathering a variety of information about me, she asked if I had a partner. Thinking I hadn't heard her correctly I asked her to repeat herself. When once again she asked me this question, I immediately began to cry and stammer and tell her that no, I no longer had a partner because he had died last Thanksgiving. Since he had been a client of God's Love, I wanted to give something back to the organization. I had clearly embarrassed her as she apologized and said that that wasn't what she had meant. She was only inquiring if I had someone with whom I was going to partner up with for delivering the meals. I laughed and apologized to her for over-reacting. We both laughed as she told me that hearing what I had just told her, she understood why I had reacted in the way I did.

Almost all of my close friends called at some point on Thanksgiving to let me know they were thinking of me and inquiring about how I was doing. I cooked dinner at my friend Ed's house, and was glad of the activity to keep me busy and distracted. Yet I was very tense, and never relaxed that day. The following day was the actual first-year anniversary of Lee's death, and I decided that I needed a very personal ritual to mark the occasion. I bought a Jewish memorial candle–a Yahrtzeit candle–and lit it in front of a photo collage of Lee I brought into my living room. Several times during the day, I'd go look at that collage, or the photos in our album, reread his letters and cards to me, play sad songs and cry. All of this felt very special and wonderful as I wanted to be alone with what ever feelings came up. I cried often that day, the first time was when I called his mom in Georgia. In the late afternoon, I felt completely exhausted and fell asleep for four hours. The day somehow disappeared and seems a blur. I slept well that night and had dreams full of Lee. The following morning, I awoke incredibly refreshed and energetic. Doing a power work-out at the gym, I felt as if I had really turned a corner.

Integrating what it's like to live in a world where Lee isn't just a phone call or few minutes away is a continuous chore. My love affair with Lee, his illness and death have greatly changed me, challenging me to grow beyond my wildest expectations. My time as a widower who was actively grieving while still going on with his life continuously challenged me in unexpected ways. I don't have the answers, and felt extremely haunted by the intensity and pervasiveness of mourning my beloved friend and partner. Yet, the ultimate challenge for me was to rediscover and reinvent myself. A few days after the anniversary, I finally decided to take off the wedding band that Lee had given me. Initially, my finger both looked and felt naked without the gold band that I had worn for more than three years. The fact that even weeks after I removed the ring, there was still an indentation in the skin on the ring finger of my left hand seemed a perfect metaphor for how I was feeling. Removing the ring made me feel as if I was freeing myself from something holding me back. I began to feel a bridge to my still uncertain future, a future to meet men without my wearing a symbol of another relationship, a future filled with possibilities as well as memories.

Nineteen months after Lee died, I felt a need to visit his parents and see his grave, and flew down to south Georgia. While on the telephone with his mother the day before the visit, giving her the details of my flight arrival she tearfully said to me in a quivering voice, "This is going to be an upbeat visit, isn't it." This made me nervous, since I was filled with a slew of feelings on the eve of my journey. Thinking about what she said, I realized that what she was telling me was not to expect that she could emotionally take care of me. I spent the time on the flight down thinking a lot about Lee and how far I had come in the past nineteen months. During his lifetime, I had never expected to be making the trip we had so often shared alone, without him. I felt a bit dissociated from myself, but I was also looking forward to seeing these people who always had embraced me, welcomed me lovingly into their lives and expressed nothing but appreciation for how I had cared for their son.

The visit was an emotion-filled time. His mother and I cried as we embraced at the airport both on my arrival and departure. Standing at Lee's grave and looking at the headstone in his family's plot, I had enormous difficulty connecting that burial plot with the man who had brought me the greatest happiness I had ever known. I was filled with rage that I was standing at the grave of a man 32 years old. Yet it felt right that he was buried in the welcoming embrace of his family and that his mother, brother and I cried together, as we held each other once again standing there on that sultry May evening. On the flight north I felt some real completion and closure to my grieving. I had been worried about how I would be during that visit sleeping in the bed Lee and I shared in his boyhood room. I was exhausted, and spent emotionally, but in a very satisfying way. I felt complete and finally ready to have all the love Lee brought into my life be a permanent part of my being, even while the ashes of his body would permanently remain in the south he both loved and had to escape.

Postcard from Grief

Craig Lucas

My lover died this year on January 5th. We were together for 11 years. He was 40. His name was Timothy Scott Melester. He was a surgeon and an AIDS educator.

I find my way by sticking to simple declarative sentences: hand holds over the swampy, rocky terrain of my terror and grief. After the initial crush of letters and flowers, phone calls and devotional meals, I went into a mania of work–writing plays and screenplays, attending rehearsals, traveling, seeing friends, tackling projects. I went through all of Tim's belongings and gave many of them away. I took off my wedding ring.

Now, 7 months after the fact, the layers of shock are beginning to fall away and I am left with a feeling for which nothing in my life has prepared me: not religion, not politics, not philosophy. I have stopped running, and the waves are breaking over me in no regular pattern, each one bringing new sensations and stripping me further of my illusions: I know nothing about who I am, where I am going, what I believe, what I want. Tim was my anchor: his battle to live was my battle.

My closets and bookshelves are filled with his notes and text-books from medical school. What happened to all that learning and effort? Where did it go? The four languages he taught himself to speak, and the two dead ones he learned to read–all the facts,

Craig Lucas is the author of several plays and screenplays, including *Long Time Companion* and *Prelude to a Kiss*. "Postcard from Grief" was originally published in *The Advocate*, October 3, 1995, Issue 691, and is reprinted with permission.

[Haworth co-indexing entry note]: "Postcard from Grief." Lucas, Craig. Co-published simultaneously in *Journal of Gay & Lesbian Social Services* (The Haworth Press, Inc.) Vol. 7, No. 2, 1997, pp. 29-31; and: *Gay Widowers: Life After the Death of a Partner* (ed: Michael Shernoff) The Haworth Press, Inc., 1997, pp. 29-31; and: *Gay Widowers: Life After the Death of a Partner* (ed: Michael Shernoff) The Harrington Park Press, an imprint of The Haworth Press, Inc., 1997, pp. 29-31.

the growing up, the struggle and ultimate joy of coming out to his friends and family, all the music he listened to, all the novels he devoured: where are they now? So much wisdom and beauty and pain–vanished. Friends put me in touch with a medium and she convinced me that his spirit was present. Every word she spoke on his behalf was plausible. She knew countless things she couldn't have known. So perhaps our spirits do go on. Still I can't touch him, I can't kiss him, I can't suck, fuck and hold him. He can't reach up and stop me from picking my nose.

Nothing makes any sense to me. I have stopped reading the *New York Times*: it's all gossip, fashion and obscene cruelty I have no power to change. In the months since Tim died, the world is still obsessed with O. J. Simpson. I turn on the TV less than once a week, and I want to vomit.

I talk to Tim. Out loud. I attend my support group, and continue to write, and to see friends. Others who are grieving share their experiences with me–online, in person, even by snail mail. The depth of their despair is the air I breathe. Here are other things I enjoy: Sad music. Sex of almost any kind–cyber, phone, video voyeurism, even real and true in the flesh sex. Nature–watching the sunset, walking in a garden, on the beach, playing with my dogs. They understand my grief perfectly, it would seem, and when I cry, they grow still and pensive, put their faces on my knee and wait for me to come out of it. Which is more than most people can do. A very few friends and colleagues are able to listen when I howl, to be present and hold my hand, or make me laugh. But the most common response to my litany of boundless sorrow is, "So what does your shrink say?" Anyone who says that to me can expect to be deleted from my address book. Grief is not a pathology. It is the body's natural response to devastation. Anyone who can formulate a stiff upper lip is, to me, already dead. I mourn for them. Go away if you can't stand my grief. It's nowhere near over.

My rage is boundless, too. I want Bill Clinton to lose in the next election and I am going to actively campaign against him. I will consider voting for anyone who steps forward and says that Bill Clinton has failed miserably; he is a cowardly fuck who can't even be bothered to file a brief in the Supreme Court opposing Colorado's Amendment Two and should be dragged through the streets of every city and town, like Mussolini, weeping while we pelt him with rotten *FRUIT* to remind him of who elected him.

That's just the tip of the iceberg. Don't tell me I'm lucky to be alive, to be HIV negative. Don't tell me that life is beautiful. Don't tell me that I have a lot to offer. To whom? A nation that wants to lower taxes on the rich as it abandons the poor and disenfranchised to further deprivation? A culture that accepts a filthy, reactionary piece of crap like *Pulp Fiction* and calls it Art?

Here's what I understand: people who tear at their flesh and throw themselves in the grave. People who join monasteries and spend the rest of their days praying for peace. Terrorists.

Maybe I'll come out of this and be utterly ashamed to have confessed to the depths of what I am experiencing. Maybe, some-day, I will marry another wonderful man and we'll adopt a child and name him Tim. Or maybe I will decide that the countless deaths I have witnessed are too much for me, that the consolations of sex and music and art and love and community are not enough in the face of this idiot culture, this drug-besotted land of ours, filled with death and indifference. And I will join my loved ones "before my time." Don't ask me what my shrink says.

People who are not grieving say "Don't get depressed, *orga-nize!*" Of course they're right. I hope to be back in the ranks of the mentally balanced. But I do not believe I can get there without being here first. So here I am. This is my postcard from Grief. Don't write. Wish I weren't here.

Excerpts from a Diary

Stephen Greco

By coincidence, the transformation of my dear, departed lover, Barry, into "my first husband" started a year, to the day, after he died. It was an evening in the fall of 1988, and I had cooked an elaborate dinner for a guy I was sort of interested in, at home, in the apartment Barry and I had shared for twelve years. Reclining in exactly the spot where Barry died, on a daybed in the living room, this guy and I fell into a long and passionate embrace that caused me, as its repercussions expanded over the next several months, to reexamine most of the ideas I had held for three decades about men, about love, about Life Itself. I hadn't set out to reexamine anything that evening. I only wanted to kiss someone–and to counteract, for one more day, the southern Italian brand of widowhood that had made such an strange impression on me as a child: the wearing of black; the lighting of candles; the endless veneration of faded snap-shots of glossy-haired war heroes, in frames tucked with bits of palm. I'd decided instead–indeed, planned, during Barry's year-long defeat by AIDS–to be the kind of widower whom everyone might admire for being "strong" enough to keep looking forward, instead of dwelling on the past. Whatever that means.

The new guy was someone I'll call "A," and I remember won-

Stephen Greco, a former editor of *Interview* and *The Advocate*, is the author of the short story "The Last Blowjob," included in *Best Gay Erotica* 1996. He lives in New York.

[Haworth co-indexing entry note]: "Excerpts from a Diary." Greco, Stephen. Co-published simultaneously in *Journal of Gay & Lesbian Social Services* (The Haworth Press, Inc.) Vol. 7, No. 2, 1997, pp. 33-42; and: *Gay Widowers: Life After the Death of a Partner* (ed: Michael Shernoff) The Haworth Press, Inc., 1997, pp. 33-42; and: *Gay Widowers: Life After the Death of a Partner* (ed: Michael Shernoff) The Harrington Park Press, an imprint of The Haworth Press, Inc., 1997, pp. 33-42. Single or multiple copies of this article are available for a fee from The Haworth Document Delivery Service [1-800-342-9678, 9:00 a.m. - 5:00 p.m. (EST). E-mail address: getinfo@ haworth.com].

dering, when he decided to install himself on the daybed after dinner, (a) whether we'd kiss, and (b) what Barry would have thought of the new fabric I'd chosen to recover the cushions. Among the cushions, by the way, was a fuzzy toy kitten that someone had given to Barry either in the hospital or during his final few weeks at home. (I mentioned none of this to A.) People brought Barry lots of stuffed animals, and after the funeral I gave most of them away, to dying friends and infant nephews. But I kept the kitten because it had reminded Barry and me of our own, short-haired silver tabby, Farquhar, who died (Jesus!) two weeks before Barry did. I was an editor of a magazine at the time, and there were plenty of men to go out with when I finally felt like doing that again–though at first, unconsciously, I kind of edited out all the prospects who were too different from Barry. Where were all the thirty-five year, balding, muscular, Jewish writer/producers, I wanted to know. Then a friend suggested I should cast my nets wider–and suddenly there was A, who worked in the same office. He was taller, skinnier, much younger than me, and basically straight, though subtly attuned to recent progress in male sexual identity which my marriage had somehow prevented me from appreciating.

Some of the entries from my journal that were written during the year when Barry was dying were published in the *European Gay Review*, then reprinted in the book, *Personal Dispatches: Writers Confront AIDS*. So it seemed logical, when I was asked to contribute something to this collection, that I look through the entries from the following year, to see if there were evidence of a heart opening up after a grave blow–of a man deciding how and why to try love again. There was such evidence, and here it is.

7-4-88

Afternoon nap. I dream of Barry. We were talking, then I realized that he'd died–which, I suppose, is why I was telling him about my loneliness and the boy I'd been making love to moments before– lithe, smooth, small. In the dream, I started wailing. Barry just looked at me.

7-18-88

Suddenly I feel I'm not blindly looking for another husband. I'm *dating*, which people tell me is the only possible way to see if someone attractive is remotely worthy of being my mate. With Barry, I just knew.

8-3-88

I miss being in love. And now that I'm single again, I've never been so depressed about the quality of gay life in New York. Is this all we've built?

9-9-88

Rangely, with Susan and Harriet. We're all sad and depressed. Shortly after arriving at the cabin and puzzling absently over evidence of alterations, I realize it's the same one Barry and I stayed in, in 1975. Honeymoon memories come swimming back slowly, as I walk around outside, examining the cabin's foundations and its orientation on the site; and in the bathroom, as I reach for a towel and register the position of the rack I once claimed, with beastly inconnubiality, as "my own." The hot water pipe clanks now the way it did then, but only after the second or third clank was I sure I remembered this.

9-10-88

Not to scatter, is what we've decided. Rangely is fairly undeveloped and likely to remain so for a while, but what if we return here in five years and find that the lovely blueberry patch I had in mind has been turned into a condo? Early in the morning we rented a boat and rowed out into the middle of the lake, all bright sun, basking gulls, brisk breeze, occasional seaplanes. After resting for a moment–during which I thought about how little I've actually swum in these frigid waters–we unsealed the box and took the plastic bag into our hands. Then each of us took turns scooping ashes out of the bag and slipping them overboard, where they sank into the crystal depths in a cloud of sparkles. The fish appeared to sense nothing special as

Barry's elements returned to nature. Unceremoniously I emptied the rest of the bag (except for a small amount I wanted to keep with me) and then did the same with Farquhar's remains. Later, we looked around town and bought a few things—wool, handmade horn buttons, organic produce for the evening meal.

9-20-88

A to dinner last night. The "Lasagne of Seductive Evil"—so-dubbed by Felice Picano—proved more potent than I'd hoped. This morning, A was improvising on the piano when I came out of the shower . . .

9-21-88

I'm drastically love-sick. Alternatively, the world is all hope for me, then all despair. At the office I'm trying to maintain the distance he's asked for, but I get queasy when I wonder if the request has more to do with some kind of fear than with simple discretion. Of course he's young, as friends remind me, and all of this—the gay stuff, the age difference, simple affection—might be very new for him.

9-24-88

We're supposed to do something Monday night. I won't think about anything else until then. In fact, I'm a wreck, and constantly trying to figure out how I got this way. Was it only at the end of August that A came to intern at the magazine? "Dark and stormy," was the way our managing editor describe him. I thought he was sort of cute, and despite my reservations about his age and our respective positions (and what may have been a certain hostility on his part when I began to float past his desk a little too often), I let myself become enamored—though I was too nervous, at first, even to ask him to lunch. But we started talking, about whatever. Then one day after work, somewhere right at the beginning of September, a bunch of us went for a drink at Sugar Reef, after which he, Kiki, and I found ourselves at the Duplex, of all places. He wound up toasting his new friends, which touched me, but still, as we sat there nursing gin-and-tonics, listening to sad/happy bar anthem after sad/happy bar anthem, he seemed a bit distant. We had lunch a few days after that, just the two of us, which I clumsily instigated; and on the 7th we went for a beer after work–his idea. He writes, plays the guitar, draws cartoons that are populated with these mordant little stick figures. Talk was becoming a bit more personal, yet I had no way of knowing whether an advance of intimacy would be welcome. And somehow I'd begun to be secure enough in his friendship that I thought it might be no great problem if I made such an advance and it were gently rebuffed. On the 13th there was dinner at his place, with a couple of his friends from London; on the 14th, he joined Amy and me at the Met for the Boccioni show, then tagged along with us to the McLaren opening, after which he came with me to Paul Zaloom and later to McManus's for a drink, over which I got The Life Story. The Bessies were on the 15th and then there was dinner at my place on the 19th. Now what?

9-27-88

Another of life's firsts for me. Last night, after inquiring whether he was going to stay over at my place again, I got the "father figure" speech. Which I took as a no.

9-28-88

The good news is that I'm going to live. Dr. William says that the mucous that has kept me clearing my throat constantly for the last two weeks is merely a reaction to my drinking too much milk. The bad news is that I've got nothing to live for.

10-10-88

Tea with George [Whitmore], at his place. He's skinny and moving kind of slow, but otherwise pretty much the same. He fears forgetting things . . .

10-14-88

A late-night, phone JO session with a man chanting "Kill, kill, kill . . ." Fun, really. These things are not half as bizarre as they sound.

Obviously, this guy and I are both the kind of homos who wear bow ties and suspenders and go to the opera.

10-16-88

Sorting through Robert [Ferro]'s and Michael [Grumley]'s things this morning, with Robert's sisters. Daunted at first by the prospect of pulling apart a life's work of collection and composition—the books, papers, objects, artworks, curios, and examples of historic hand tailoring that the boys kept in several hundred thousand proper places around those five rooms—we begin digging things out of closets and drawers and packing them up. Everything's being stored for now. Dismantling an apartment is much more horrifying than seeing someone physically waste away. At least with disease you can get some compensatory fortifications of the spirit. No word from A.

10-19-88

It's midnight and we're rattling downtown on the #1 train after seeing Giulio Cesare. Since I still have to practice my reading from Second Son for tomorrow's memorial service, I don't really have time for a drink. A is probably relieved. Anyway, he's serving up some kind of exuberant sweetness. Patiently answering his puppy-ish questions, I fixate on that long, muscular neck and wonder whether I'll ever kiss it again.

10-27-88

I believe the term to describe what A and I are doing together is "hanging out." But I'm not sure it's the most efficient thing for me to be doing at this point in my life. He did show up at the big Spy party I invited him to, but blitzed on acid. He proceeded to navigate ahead of me through the crowd, singing and ranting and philoso-phizing, not unmagnificently; then he disappeared, leaving me to wonder if he'd passed out behind some potted palm, let alone to handle the most acutely painful rejection I've felt in a long time. He called shortly after I got home, from somewhere, with a paltry explanation. I screamed at him and hung up.

10-29-88

Nothing yesterday or today. We were supposed to go to John Kelly tonight. Then I call his apartment and learn from a roommate that he's gone to Kingston to visit his mother.

11-29-88

La Vie Parisienne last night, at the New York Academy. Even as we were having a drink before the performance, A was checking his watch. He never wears a watch. "Got a date?" I inquired with gentle sarcasm. And then he smiled sheepishly and said he sort of did. Fucking Christ, I thought, what is this guy thinking about? It's someone he met while looking for a sublettor, he explained–a girl he somehow just doesn't want to lose touch with. "Don't be upset," he said. "It's apples and oranges." "I don't care that it's a girl, A," I said. "But how can you just check out like that after we spend an evening together?" But I did care. I would have been even more upset if it were a boy. Limply, he tried to apply a little charm. "Don't worry," he smiled. "She'll probably blow me off and tell me to go find some handsome, older editor." Yeah, sure. Asshole. The performance was brilliant, the best we've seen together. During the intermission, in order to avoid everyone in the audience (including the producer and my own music critic), I steered him toward the stairwell, where we had one of those conversations in which one person makes a series of angry comments and the other tries to say nothing in particular in an annoyingly pleasant, superficial way. I wound up, after a glass of wine, poking my finger into his sternum and reminding him that he makes me crazy. And I think he might have liked that, because it was then he admitted that everyone he's ever loved has treated him like shit. Back in our seats, just before the second act, I decided that he might simply be trying to force my hand. Perhaps I have been wrong to adore him so un-coercively, I thought; perhaps I should be playing dirtier. So I turned to him and said, "Look, just don't go. I want you to be with me tonight." "No, I have to go," was the reply. "I want to, Stephen." Which made me ponder, as I sat back in my seat, what my life has come to, recently, that I should be delivered such a statement. Is A the right one for me to be making extravagant plays for? Should someone in his late thirties, freshly widowered, be making extravagant plays for anyone? This particular Offenbach, even done gloriously, seemed the wrong music to accompany such thoughts. But as the second act perked along, I did understand something. I can hardly still imagine myself married in spirit to Barry if I am throwing myself so intensively at someone else. It must be time to remove the wedding rings–something, I should add, that I'd been considering doing ever since the anniversary of Barry's death, two months ago. Quietly, in my lap–but of course hoping that A would see–I pulled off the two gold bands that Barry and I had bought for each other at R. J. White on Christopher Street, and slipped them into my shirt pocket. Afterwards, a stony walk to the cash machine on LaGuardia Place. Homeless guys everywhere, to each of whom A offers a few words, or a cigarette, or the hand signal Churchill used to flash to mean victory, which now seems to indicate a much vaguer thing, peace. We're standing there. Should he never call again, he asks. Good question, I say. "Well, I'm going to call and you can be the one to hang up if you want," he says. "Oh, A," I drawl. "I won't hang up." We hug, and he goes off. Then I walk all the way over to Seventh Avenue before hailing a cab, deciding over and over again that it's jazz I'm going to put on when I get home, not New Age . . .

12-12-88

Back from Brussels. Mark [Morris]'s L'Allegro a masterpiece. I don't support A's smoking at all, but I've brought him back a selection of unfiltered European cigarettes and am signing the note, "C. Everett Koop."

12-25-88

As soon as I get to Ellenville I go to the hospital. Uncle John is sitting in the hallway with Grandma Kitty, who's been waiting for a place in the county home for months now. Slumped over and looking deeply dazed–no, more distracted, as Barry seemed to be during those last days–she has to be reminded who I am and says nothing without being prompted. Uncle John looks tired. He visits her every day and today has already been there for hours, making small talk with the nurses and tending devotedly to his stepmother. When he discovers a puddle of urine under Grandma Kitty's wheelchair, he automatically sets about blotting it up with a towel. What will happen to him when he gets old, he wonders aloud. Dinner in Kerhonkson with my sister's in-laws. As soon afterwards as I can, I drive to Kingston. They are all there—A's mom and her lover; his dad and his lover; A's best friend "J," a sweet boy A obviously loves (but who has a girlfriend, A contrives to inform me); the sister, who comes in later with her boyfriend; the two dogs, Rocky and Putz. The house is a century old and decorated in the warm, eccentrically hit-and-miss, extended-family manner that my high school girlfriend's was; and it's a pleasure to be welcomed among all these nice people, even if A seems a little blank. He takes me upstairs to show me the attic room he's converted into his living-slash-work space, lends me some tapes, shows me some of the writing he's been doing. Then later, downstairs, coffee and pie are served. After some pleasantly generic holiday chatter, it's time for me to go, since I have to be back at Uncle John's by midnight. Cordial farewells. A says he can walk me to the car and have a cigarette at the same time. Outside, my thank-yous, then he explains the meaning of a few comments I thought I'd overheard about a trip out west. He's "sort of" going to Seattle with J, and driving back cross-country in maybe three months. We're standing in a dead-quiet street, next to my sister's beat-up Citation, in which he de-clined to sit as we talk. It's, like, 30 degrees. I study my shoes, then tell him that I love him. Oh, he knows all about that, he says brightly, but he hasn't wanted to "disappoint" me. In a touchingly well-rehearsed manner, he suggests that he just can't love me as I might want him to. When he comes to New York, in a few days, we'll talk about it. And that's a promise, he says. The drive back to Ellenville is dark and silent. What keeps coming back to me is the image of two men with semi-concealed razor blades I saw lurking at the bottom of the elevator in the Clark Street subway station early this morning, as I was leaving Brooklyn with a bunch of other holiday travelers. I called the 84th Precinct from a pay phone, but have been, shamefully, less horrified all day than I might have been. Do I even belong on this planet any more, now that Barry's gone? I write these words in the Spring Street apartment house to which I was brought home on the second day of my life. Uncle John's asleep in his bedroom downstairs, off the dining room–which, as I kid, I always thought was a weird place for a bedroom, though my sister and I liked that that's where the presents were to be found when the family gathered for Christmas dinner. He never married, Uncle John. Neither did my late Aunt Mary, whose room he's put me in for the night. Her white china, 50s-moderne statue of the Blessed Virgin watches over me. The twin bed is uncomfortably narrow and the last few minutes of Christmas 1988 tick away. Dear Aunt Mary, I pray, can't you do something to help your poor Stephen?

1-3-89

He hasn't called. He won't.

1-5-89

Wow. A fine talk, honest and affectionate, over tequila and beer at McManus's. He apologized for the night of the Spy party and said that he didn't know whether or not I would believe him, but that he loves me dearly. Sigh. And that he wants to join a band again so I will know a rock star. Nobody's ever said such a tender thing to me. Amazingly, we wind up in Brooklyn and he spends the night–on the couch. This morning, I squeeze some of the oranges my parents sent me, while we discuss having dreamed about each other . . .

1-7-89

Today he leaves for Seattle.

1-13-89

On a whim yesterday, I substituted the word "loverboy" for the name "Adam," in the last few months of my journal. Then I did the same with "Mr. Buttwipe." The computer makes these things easy. The exercise was much funnier than I thought it would be.

No Return

Winston Wilde

I was asked one night, "Does it *feel* like a year since Paul died?"

Yes, it feels like a year. It feels like a lifetime, a year that has been a journey of soul searching and soul making, of loneliness and terror, of joy and erotic rampage.

Being in a loving relationship with a reflecting companion gives one a window into his own soul. My pane has been shattered. Dutifully I've swept up the shards and put them in the recycling bin. But a great wind has scattered the slivers about, ten thousand invisible land mines from a war now long lost, lying in wait for unpredictable moments of fresh blood. My lover is gone, and with him I lost my point of reference, the reliable reassurance of unconditional love and adoration. Our *pas de deux*–that anchor of our counterbalance–has ended.

After fourteen years in two successive relationships, I found myself having to learn again how to monkey through the junglegym of the singles' playground. The rules have been changed in the midst of this plague–too many corpses and fears–and I have changed, too, having been struck by the arrows of love. When I was last single it was a happier time for gay people. Now I see the psychic carnage of Republican indifference, and worse even, our

Winston Wilde is a laughing pervert bodybuilder who reads between sets, drives like a maniac, meditates and loves with all his broken heart who lives in Los Angeles.

[Haworth co-indexing entry note]: "No Return." Wilde, Winston. Co-published simultaneously in *Journal of Gay & Lesbian Social Services* (The Haworth Press, Inc.) Vol. 7, No. 2, 1997, pp. 43-58; and: *Gay Widowers: Life After the Death of a Partner* (ed: Michael Shernoff) The Haworth Press, Inc., 1997, pp. 43-58; and: *Gay Widowers: Life After the Death of a Partner* (ed: Michael Shernoff) The Harrington Park Press, an imprint of The Haworth Press, Inc., 1997, pp. 43-58. Single or multiple copies of this article are available for a fee from The Haworth Document Delivery Service [1-800-342-9678, 9:00 a.m. - 5:00 p.m. (EST). E-mail address: getinfo@haworth.com].

being silenced by the moronic Big Mac Baptist Democrat. We've been lied to and betrayed as we die by the hundreds of thousands. Like Indians. Like Jews. Countless tens of thousands of my gay brothers are "in recovery," battered by alienation and self-doubt, broken-hearted for lack of love alone. I see the ruin of my people, the relics of my noble tribe, and I am amazed that any of us–yes, so many of us–are able to find love and companionship.

The following fragments of stories were written over many months and are immune to chronology. The past is very present, there is no future, and now is but an opportunity for renewal.

***

"You must tell people about us, Winnie," Paul implored me several times in his last year. He said our people needed to hear about the magic we have. Gay people need to hear about our love stories. Love stories of disabled people, battered by life's woeful countenance. We are a strong people, a people who rise up, without warning, enraptured with romance and dreams made real. Tell them about love during the plague, he said. Tell them how we made love between the bombs. Tell about our struggles and how we overcame them, about the myth we enact.

Still, I am conflicted as I begin this epistle: Do I follow Paul's wishes or observe my preferred devotional silence? Inside I feel like an Indian who thinks it no good to speak of the dead. Outside, that dominant culture keeps pushing at me, pulling, *Tell us of the immortal beloved.* Besides, Paul was the writer, not me. I'm good at living life, not writing about it. I've been struggling for nine months with the words to put on his headstone. (I begged Paul for four years to write his epitaph. Now I see why he didn't. He knew that I could get away with a more flattering narrative than he could.)

How much of what I am writing to you is me as the grieving widow, how much as the recovering self? How much do I hear Paul? What fragments of me or of Paul-and-me survive? I don't know. I am told that writing this could be a therapeutic process, "cathartic." But I fear when one discusses spiritually empowered events their magical properties can diminish. Nevertheless, romantic love has a dharma which includes compromise, often throws caution to the wind and at times unreasoningly jumps forward. So, I do.

Whoever you are, beware I have no answers. Why do you want to read this, I wonder. Probably because you admired Paul Monette the writer. Paul received hundreds of fan letters–all positive (and he answered almost every one of them)–thanking him for the honesty and sensitivity in his writings, often declaring that his books changed their lives–straights as well as gays. I saw people at his book signings unable to speak, muted in sorrow or overcome with tears of despair. Perhaps you were fortunate enough to have met or known Paul Monette the person. He was kind to everyone. Paul was encouraging to the outlandish and creative, compassionate with the feeble-minded and the illiterate. He invigorated people with passionate dialogue: from politics with cab drivers around the world, to murder mystery plots with doormen and bellhops. And a fortunate few may have been acquainted with Paul's great perv mind, truly of the highest order. But whoever you are, I invite you in to some very personal statements I am about to make. They are not all pretty. AIDS is not pretty.

***

Last Wednesday was our anniversary–the big one, the day we met. I went to Forest Lawn to visit my dead guys, and as always, worried on the drive there that either someone would be at Paul's grave or that no one would be there. An older woman was there, sitting, holding vigil with a stack of Paul Monette books.

Hey you! I thought, Get off of my cloud. *It's our anniversary, lady. I want to be alone with my husband.* As I approached, I saw that she was indignant with the same territorial imperative. With my California smile and an outstretched hand I offered, "Good Afternoon. My name is Winston." Well, I thought she was going to wither into the grass with humility. This sprightly grandmother explained that she doesn't usually visit graves. I told her that I hadn't either, until Paul taught me to.

She started to cry. I asked her why. She said, "Today is the day I met my husband, 50 years ago." So, after all, she was the perfect person to be there.

***

When I returned home from Paul's memorial service I removed my wedding band that Paul bought for me at Tiffany's. I don't know why. I looked around inside our home which was practically wall-papered with photographs of the two of us: at parties and grave-yards, in Rome, in Tahiti, in black-tie and leather, at our wedding, in love, always in love. And in every room and hallway these remind-ers of loss were shouting at me, *Look at how happy we were.* Look at what we've lost. I unhung every last image of the two of us. In minutes all the photos were down and stacked in the attic. I was determined to not become immobilized like an acquaintance, wid-owed now eighteen months, who has yet to begin dispatching his dead lover's clothes.

For the first time in my life, politics and current events were no longer of interest. I canceled the *New York Times*, the *Los Angeles Times*, the *New York Review of (each other's) Books*. The not too personal *New Yorker* self-stopped. I felt a great need to simplify my life. In need of an empty room, I gave away every stick of living room furniture. I didn't know why, just did what I had to do. The scary success of motion felt better than the safe glue of inertia. It was a good time to edit my rolodex.

Whether it was altruism or mania, I had made Paul the primary purpose of my life for four years. I worshiped him and ferociously protected him. In that way, I was his daddy. He was my purpose, my function, my reality. We died.

***

I am supposed to be sharing with you how I am coping with being a widower. But I am unable to discuss how I am doing without reflecting on Paul. Paul and me. Still so much of my identi-ty is wrapped up in Paul-and-me. We had a fabulous life together. This process to find myself is painful and poses a conflict of inter-est. Does it have to be that each step I take towards my own ground of being equates to taking a step away from Paul? I can't help but hold onto my thoughts of Paul; *today is his birthday, tomorrow is the day we met, we were in Paris at this time.* The holidays are coming. Paul loved Christmas. I heard him bravely warn, "This is probably my last Christmas," during *five* Christmases. What will I do without my drama queen, my laughing man, my love? I am dreading this holiday season. I refuse to buy a single gift nor step an inch into any shopping complex. I will not listen to one goddamn carol: no tree, no lights, no parties, no fun. I am going to have an awful time out of respect for my dead lover.

***

I held him dead in my arms. We lay in an altered state. I wondered, *What do I do with me now? What is my role? Lover of whom?* The future is precarious for the servant whose master is gone. Holding Paul, my eyes landed on his night stand. Ativan. Xanax. Morphine. MS Contin. Dalmane. Elavil. Tylenol with codeine. Calmly, fearlessly, I recognized a window of opportunity. Everyone's gone, I thought. I could down all of these right now and end this life of struggle and triumph, of pain and love. If there is an afterlife, I could go with him. But I was cautious and hesitated. At times I regret that I didn't pop those pills. It would have been a swift and tidy ending.

I am mad that he is dead. I am out of my mind with rage and grief. In tradition, I rent the lapel of my jacket for the funeral. I am insane with jealousy for people who have outlived Paul. It's not pretty. I see certain people and wish them dead instead of Paul. My judgments are ruthless. What is that crippled old man doing on the park bench? He should be dead, not Paul. What is that fat homeless woman doing having children? Look at that bimbo *shiksa* next to me on the freeway, checking her fake nails while laughing into her god damn cell phone. Hang up and drive, bitch. You should be dead, not Paul.

I've never claimed any peaceful Zen saintliness. I'm much too impassioned.

***

Phase I, the first few weeks, I kept so busy it was really easy to cope. Detached from current events and certainly from the intricate machinations of the virus and all who are ravaged by it, both in body and in soul, I retreated. I was frothing and inconsolable. I stayed home.

On Kings Road I turned my empty living room into a shrine for Paul. In my memory of Paul I found continuity, serenity. I dreaded leaving the house and engaging my features of agoraphobia. Only by reclaiming Paul and Paul-and-me could I find a point of balance. At home I recalled our last days together. They were blessed with magic.

***

For about three months I was in Phase II, in which I was freaking out about being alone. Eating alone, sleeping alone, channel surfing, talking out loud to myself, going everywhere in the car alone, masturbating alone. I couldn't bear to eat alone, again, and again and again, but there was no one I wanted to eat with. Scores of invitations, but I didn't want to eat with anyone. I wanted to eat with my lover. I wanted to eat with Paul and watch him smoosh food all over his face, knock over the salt and pepper and helplessly hand me the ketchup to open and pour for him. I wanted to see him stand up and drop his napkin to the floor again. I wanted to bathe in his kind and exuberant voice as he engaged others in conversation.

I wasn't eating. Sometimes it was 4:00 in the afternoon before I realized that I'd not eaten a thing all day. Nothing sounded appealing. Nothing tasted good. I didn't feel whole enough to be wanting to eat anything anyway. How could I expect to enjoy food without Paul? Holding Paul heavily in my heart, and having been trained to not begin eating until everyone has been served, proved anorexically paradoxical. Food was such a huge part of our shared joy. We loved our food.

In that difficult period of Phase II which seemed to last forever, I was terribly lonely. I realized how much for granted I took being touched. Paul and I touched and kissed and hugged every day. We said "I-Love-You's," "I-need-you's"—and other endearments too personal to reveal—to each other every day of our four years, two months and three weeks. The throngs had died down and too few were hugging me or kissing me. Forget the endearments. *Someone, please, touch me.* I felt like one of those monkeys in a glass cubicle, everyone outside looking in, only a carpet remnant for a mother. Two weeks could pass and all I got were a few handshakes at the gym. I needed to be touched, kissed, rubbed, fondled, fucked with, ears licked, hair pulled, heart massaged, loved by a gentle fat hairy Pan. I dreamt. I dreamt of sacred muscle brothers from my sanctuary the gym, and of the men from our queer streets. These virile sissy beings blossomed into nocturnal archetypes: the bearded receiver, the booted blond, the lactating man. Lost in a swirl of loving manliness, without anchor, I drifted and dreamt of great manly love. I wanted a Zeus, hirsute and ten feet tall, in a police uniform, to swoop his big hands way down into my proverbial sandbox, enrapture me from the rear, and as I swoon we sail upwards and he says gently, "Don't worry, little boy, I'll take care of you. I'm sorry you've been lost. But now I will protect you and keep you, and you will live among the gods."

I was willing to compromise: he could be any height, smooth, even ungodly. But the uniform was a must.

I feel ripe with potential for love. I park myself at local coffee houses reading and people-watching. Every day I see magnificent gentlemen passerby, all sizes, shades and ages, and I think, *I could love that man.* I could let that man love me. Look at that black guy who's smiling with pure joy: I could love him. Look at that Roman god with three days growth, gesticulating over his espresso: I could love him. Everywhere in West Hollywood—at the gas station, the post office, the car wash, Pavilions—I fall in love. I ask myself, Why can't I just be happy with being alone? I remember Paul's story about, "Somebody, please find me!" I've learned from my experience with Paul that the best way to grieve the loss of a lover is to get a new one right away. Luck is not always with us though. And like acquiring riches, love is part luck. If my love-luck didn't die with Paul, it's at least dormant. How difficult it is to let it rest. Meanwhile I sip my tea or toss back a brewski, pose and wait. Watch out! There goes a Viking on roller blades!

Seriously, though, I've never been so possessed with needing love. Love has always been in my life, like tributaries weaving in and out. So why is this questing for love so omnipotent in my everyday interactions?

Being single again, I am sadly reminded of how the world separates the singles from the couples. Couples hold a revered status and get special treatment. Couples have special rights. When you are single, couplism is oppressive. Widowhood is observed as a victimization, an ill and pitiable status somewhere in the burden class of disability and emotional poverty. I am a widow. I have been demoted. Or as Bette Middler said, "I've been marked down." The widow is tragic baggage, a volatile weight that imbalances the comfortable insouciance of others. We widows cause "aesthetic anxiety" because we remind people of their own mortality and of the price of love.

Our old couple-friends take me to dinner. Every table for three is a table for four, and that empty seat is where Paul should be sitting, or could be sitting. For me, the chair is where Paul is. They are talking about a movie they saw and I am wanting to be the chair.

***

"Winston," a well-meaning dowager friend suggested, "perhaps instead of thinking of yourself as a widower, you could think of yourself as an eligible bachelor."

Eligible bachelor.

Okay. Eligible bachelor. There you have it. Now, doesn't that sound hopeful? Eligible bachelor. Okay.

How does one bachelorate? I didn't know. I'd never done it. Somehow I missed that phase. So I set about it as rationally as I could, asking myself questions of eligibility importance. *What do I have to offer? What are my assets? What kind of person would be attracted to me? What am I looking for? What will I put up with and what is out of the question? What are my mating strategies?* I'd never thought of myself as a potential spouse commodity. This was new terrain. I had been accustomed, instead, to the food-chain of gay male bodies; that cannibalistic hierarchy of looks and image. Those were my mating skills.

I was 38 years old in Phase II, and had never been on a date in my life.

Eligible bachelor was my mantra. Confidants answered my naive questions about dating etiquette. Should I bring him flowers? How do PWDs (people who date) pay the restaurant bill? Is going to a movie a stupid idea? I've listened unsympathetically for years to single people whine about their dating escapades. Never having searched for companionate love, I had no compassion for those who did.

I won't torture you with every dating fiasco during my mating month of April. But the last story is a doozy. I was on a roll. Things were looking brighter. I've always been attracted to gentlemen of a certain age, 10 to 30 years older than me, but found myself, much to my surprise, being courted by a half dozen guys from the gym in their mid-20s. It was flattering, even if it did make me feel like Ethel Merman and her cub scouts.

Spring was in the air the first week of May. I had a feeling that my luck was about to strike. I'd made dates with four different guys: Thursday night, Friday night, Saturday night and Sunday night. All gorgeous, compassionate young men. The telephone wires were sizzling with news that I was about to get laid. Thursday afternoon the Thursday night canceled. Friday evening, the Friday night and the Saturday night canceled. Mr. Sunday was supposed to call me between 5:30 and 6:00 to make plans. No word. At 6:30 I sought advice from the damn dowager who gave me the *eligible bachelor* mantra: What do I do? Do I call him? Do I not call him? What does it all mean? Are people really *this* incapable of simple human interaction?

I called Mr. Sunday and left a message that I was home and would be at home. At 7:30 he called and said he'd been shopping for tennis shoes–but didn't find any–and would be over in half an hour. An hour and a quarter later he showed up and said, "I'm really freaked out so I can't stay long. And I can't think about us having sex again."

"Don't think," I said. "Just relax. Kick back, breathe. I'll be Walt Whitman and take care of you. Put yourself in my hands." But he wouldn't. He wouldn't even hold hands or sit next to me.

That was my last date. I will not be dating again. Instead, that night, I joined a sex club, the Vortex. The next night I went to the Compound, and have since been to the King of Hearts, Hollywood Spa, Nighthawk and Cuffs. These lascivious adventures are satisfying and compelling and pornographic. But I would only be telling half the truth if I didn't mention that when I got back into my car to go home alone, I wept.

One night at the Vortex I indulged in an hour of white glove safe carnal pleasures with a tattooed Puerto Rican muscleman visiting from New York. After we shot laughing together, I told him, "I loved you tonight."

"I loved you, too." Our eyes and hearts merged for one last ovation.

Then he left, alone. Then I left, alone.

Later that night, home alone, I missed Paul something fierce. From that night on, I wear both of our wedding bands on my right hand, third finger.

At least once a week I thought to myself, Win, you don't need sex and you don't need love. What you really need is fraternity, a male utopia. And I thought of Gov. Jerry Brown (the 2nd most sexy man on the planet) and wondered if maybe I should just check-in to a Buddhist monastery for a year. Governor Brown, was it worth it? Did it help?

***

Phase III: Missing Paul terribly. Having to come to terms with being alone. I don't want to date. I don't want anyone coming over to my home. I don't want to "stay in touch" with anyone. I don't want to go out to dinner with someone so that they can feel good about taking care of the Widow Monette. As pop-psych as it sounds, I need to find out who I am. Again.

The trouble I faced was that I was in someone else's shadow for a decade before being with Paul, taking care of John and five years of his AIDS. I've been a wound-dresser for nine years, longer than our dear comrade Walt was. And now I must be alone. A voyage in quest of the self. What a challenge.

You see, the night I met Paul he'd just returned from Europe and it was about eight weeks after his lover Stephen had died. He had said in his informal lecture, "I've already been a widower and I'm not doing it again. Been there, done that. So would one of you find me a lover because I'm lonely and horny." Everyone laughed at his comment/request except me. I felt Paul's pain that night, as I am living it now.

During this gloomy phase I tired of the exhausting efforts needed to be social. I preferred the company of my dog to any human I knew. As a native Angelino who was witness to the carnage of "the industry," I've eschewed Hollywood business, gossip, folklore, and even most popular movies. They don't interest me. Like most gay men, my deceased lovers John and Paul were fond of black and white movies with Bette Davis, Joan Crawford, Talullah, and all those campy dames. At opportune moments these men drawl famous bitchy lines, and I have no clue what they're referring to. Maybe I'm missing some essential gay DNA marker. However, I did discover the musical.

Night time was the hardest time. That's when Paul and I would always have dinner together, usually make love, it was our quality time. So, at least twice a week in this widow phase I found myself perusing the musicals section at Video West. Some Italian food to go, a puff on a joint, and a whole new world was opened to me. *Carousel. South Pacific. Oklahoma! Showboat. Sweet Charity.* This was one of the healthiest steps I took in the recovery of myself from loss: I discovered something new. And musicals are almost always love stories, happy stories where people sing and dance their way through life's twists and turns.

When my life with John was dying of AIDS and I commuted daily in from Malibu, I listened a million times to a cassette of *The Sound of Music*. My favorite tune that got me through everything was Julie Andrews singing that song when she leaves the convent and is about to arrive at the Captain's mansion. She's terrified, carpetbag in one hand, guitar in the other, walking down the beautiful tree-lined path. She sings about having confidence in sunshine, confidence in rain. *And besides which, you see, I have confidence in me.* I've always meant to write her a thank you letter.

In my two months of musical mania, lasagna and tokes, I have to say that my absolute favorite discovery was *Man of La Mancha*. I rented it seven times. It's the most perfect story of all the musicals I rented. Dulcinea, who only wants love but is looked at by others only as a whore, asks Sancho Panza (Don Quixote's significant other), Why do you stay with that crazy, bumbling romantic fool?

Well, Pancho contemplates, *Because I like him*. At which point the chubby valet goes into song of why he likes Don Quixote. I think I'll rent it again tonight.

***

Every morning for the first two weeks of September I woke up crying. It appeared as though I was doing okay throughout my day, getting tasks accomplished, up to two full meals per day. I wasn't pushing a shopping cart down the street. Yet. But every morning I awoke dreading the prospect of another day without Paul. Yes, I could answer the mail, gas the car, water the yard, be responsible. But what was the point? There was no one to share life with. I was one of those isolated monkeys again. No one to care about, fuss over, devote myself to. I was lost without someone to groom: no bow-ties to straighten or ear hairs to trim. No one to leave love notes for, no one to call from random pay phones for no reason. There was no one to serve me tea in bed or worry if I was late.

And during that two week crying jag I accepted an invitation from a celebrity friend to join her at her table at the Gay Center dinner. As afternoon approached I became anxious about appearing alone—knowing her table would be in the front row—among 1500 carnivorous homosexuals. I went into the closet to get my Armani tuxedo out, and had a total hissy-fit. I threw it on the floor and stepped on it; in my mind hearing some universal psychotherapist saying, "This is inappropriate behavior, Mr. Wilde." Yelling so loudly, "*I cannot wear this without Paul*," Buddy, my dog, ran for cover. Paul and I wore our tuxedos in Paris, on cruises, at too many charity dinners, every Christmas and every Valentine's Day. The joy of it, for both of us, was the ritual of dressing each other, being each other's valet. I sobbed as I fumbled with my cufflinks realizing that John always did them before Paul. Now this middle-aged ape needs to learn a new trick: self cufflinking. I don't want to learn it. I know I'm whining: *I won't grow up*. But really, the best part of the party is when everyone goes home and you laugh and *schmooze* about it all with your lover. These tuxedo nights I realize how lonely I am, and my tears flow wild like the River Ganges.

Friends insisted I seek help. Oh please, I winced, not more goddamn therapy. I grew up in Our Village of the Queen of the Angels, progressive therapy capital of the world. I don't like therapy and I don't like therapists and I don't give a damn about where the hostility originates or ends up. Go tell someone from Auschwitz or Bosnia to modulate their anger, but leave me out. I like my anger; it's expressive and passionate and justified. So either get yourself an uzi, a white flag, or get out of my way.

"But you need to see a *grief counselor,*" my dearest friends explained. Oh, do I? I've lost over eighty friends, all of my fuckbuddies, two lovers and a dog, and I need to see a grief counselor? Where have I been? I've been grieving my Jewish guts out for fourteen years. The difference is, I realize now, I'm doing it alone. Very alone.

Still I resisted. Why would I want to grieve within some conventional formula, or join the hit parade of grief gurus? Why would I want to fit into this embarrassing culture anyway? Genet once said, "I would like the world not to change so that I can be against the world." Having more dead friends than live friends, I've decided that *my* gay community is in heaven.

I've still got my head too stuck in the sands of "grief counseling" to be able to accurately report on its value. I get painful homework to do every week: write a letter to Paul, make a list of everything I disliked about him. And for this I pay her money and *schlep* all the way to Pasadena. She says that grieving is a step-by-step process, and that I can hurry it up by accomplishing these steps more consciously. But I'm not so sure I *want* to hurry the process. Why are Americans always in such a big ass hurry? At the risk of inviting the judgment of masochism, I'm not so sure I want to stop grieving about Paul. My grief reminds me of what we had. Through my grief I hold on to the memory of Paul and to the memory of Paul-and-me. And since I don't have a lover anymore, I take great solace and joy in the memories of what was, however tortuous and agonizing the process of recollection is. It's all I've got. And I'm greedy about love, so I'll take it.

My grief counselor has been doing this for twelve years and certainly knows what she's talking about. I have learned a lot from her. But I've maneuvered through life in my own queer-ass way, never really fitting into the formulas. I think she's learning as much from me. She's counseling me in grammar, that is, present tense versus past tense.

"I'm totally freaking-out," I told her, "because Monday is Paul's birthday."

"*Would have been.*"

My windpipe closed. Tears welled up. Anger got transferred. "No. *If* Paul *would have been* here, then it *would have been* Paul's birthday. But, I *am* here and it *is* Paul's birthday."

October 16th will be Paul's birthday for the rest of my life. I think she knows that. It was her grief counselor way of delivering that soul-making sting of an emotionally braided cat. Take that, you widow. Know Thyself. Feel it and then let's go to the next plateau. We cannot progress without the pain of realization that our embodiment is moving forward, away from our past. The truth hurts.

***

Everything changed at Christmas. In a panic about being alone, I filled X-mas Eve with a cocktail party in WeHo, then a Leathermen's Saturnalia party, then a dinner given by dyke friends so I'd have somewhere to go, then the Vortex. When I awoke Christmas day, I pondered my schedule from bed: a brunch, then a movie, then a Broad Beach party, then lesbian cocktails in the Valley, dinner al fresco in Studio City, and a sex date at 10:00 p.m. I was overwhelmed with social obligations.

I got out of bed and opened the presents I'd bought and wrapped for myself, presents that Paul would have bought for me. They were on the dining room table. I was feeling totally stressed out about having to go all these places that I really didn't want to go. At brunch I decided to cancel almost everything else. I thought—*and here's the big individuation moment—I'd rather be by myself.*

I returned home. I lit the candles in the Paul Monette living room shrine. After but a brief moment of meditation, I knew exactly what to do.

At his memorial service the congregants were given paper and pencil to write their final comments to Paul. I told them that I would burn them in ceremony at a radical faerie gathering. I'd taken these notes to three gatherings but the vibe just wasn't right. Christmas was right.

I smudged the house, rang bells, rattled and drummed. I dismantled the shrine. Setting up a safe burn zone, the first paper of over 500 was lit. As I burned them one at a time, I felt as though what was written was being sung. Burning two at one time I heard harmony. As the papers burned and the room filled with swirls of smoke, gifts of greetings and love were being sung to Paul this Christmas day. I looked at random notes when I had the courage to peek through my tear-filled eyes. "Thank you for giving me life, Paul." "I'll miss you, dear friend." Smoke filled the air, activating the alarms which I had to disconnect. I burned four at once and then one to crescendo. Someone had drawn a picture of a tripartite being—human legs, jetliner wings, bird's head—soaring up from the sea at sunrise. Burned.

The noise of burning and singing and sirens and wing-flapping was not all I heard. The chairs were creaking. The rocker was rocking. The room was filled with spirits and the dead. "Dear Paul, Say hello to Michael. Tell him I'll see you guys soon." I tried to contain the ashes from floating about the room, but this was impossible. I am two-spirit, in a plane between the dead and the living.

After an hour and a half I was only about half way through. I took a break and went to Forest Lawn, blanketing red rose petals over Paul and Roger. I thought, *I wish I could see the note that I wrote to Paul, or did I burn it already?*

Back home the pyre was stoked again. "You were so important to my son, Thank you." Through the next hour of burning and tears the living room on Kings Road had its epiphany. I felt the power of reclamation.

As I sobbed at the note that I read aloud, "Go Paul, Go!" that sentient chair nearest me creaked too loud to ignore. The chair held me in my sad moment.

Late for lesbian cocktails and Studio City dinner, I hurried out the door leaving everything as it was in the living room. When I returned that night, exhausted, I went to the dining room to inspect my presents from Paul. In the middle of the table was a folded piece of paper, my note to Paul. I opened it, "I love you forever."

That was the best Christmas gift I've ever gotten.

When I wrote it I meant, *Winston loves Paul forever.* When it was given back to me on Christmas it meant to me, *Paul loves Winston forever.* For the few days before I burned it, it meant to me, *Winston must love Winston during this indefinite life.* On Christmas I unwrapped my autonomy.

I have had very little trouble with loneliness since then. I'm almost okay with being single. On New Year's Day I woke up laughing, and thanked my gods for starting my new year with a joke.

I've recovered something, now seventeen months later. I no longer wish others dead. The *Los Angeles Times* is at the stairs each morning again, not that I give a big whoopdedoo about anything inside. I've learned that I have all the criteria (and almost all the features) of Posttraumatic Stress Disorder, Chronic, and that helps put things into perspective.

I don't know where I am going, or if I will be alive in an hour. That doesn't matter. I laugh and I cry and I feel love all around me every day. My salvation is in the service of others. I am Winnie-Hanuman.

So you see, my comrades and widow mates, I have no answers. My travel-weary and war-soaked map has a hole in it. Nonetheless, there is in me some unidentified drive to muster and march and attack that evil windmill, to issue kindness when I can, to heal the souls of the wounded with adhesive love. Arriving at this impossible dream is superfluous, it is the integrity of the journey that matters. I trudge through this widow's minefield without a safety-word, and I am past the point of no return.

Tracing Time

Townsand Price-Spratlen

Is there a line to write?
Are there words to paint the hollow space?
What color is this?

"I just got out of the hospital."
"Ya. Ya. I went in on Friday, got out on Sunday night."
"I'm doin' good. Doin' good. Feelin' better, so they let me go."

I slowly opened my journal
My tears hit the blank page with a silent crash
He filled my stunned silence with words
Speaking, knowing that I could not
Simple gifts are the most powerful
Pictures of him, of us
Suddenly shout
Images that speak of a different time
Always moving, always changing

Situation and circumstance ,
Fear and self-protection

Townsand Price-Spratlen, PhD, was born in Bellingham, WA (U.S.A.), and raised in Seattle, WA. He loves the music of Nat King Cole, Regina Belle and many others, and commonly finds himself humming the melody to Phyllis Hyman's "I Refuse to Be Lonely." He has been writing poetry and short stories since junior high school, and is currently living in Columbus, OH, where he is Assistant Professor of Sociology at The Ohio State University.

[Haworth co-indexing entry note]: "Tracing Time." Price-Spratlen, Townsand. Co-published simultaneously in *Journal of Gay & Lesbian Social Services* (The Haworth Press, Inc.) Vol. 7, No. 2, 1997, pp. 59-72; and: *Gay Widowers: Life After the Death of a Partner* (ed: Michael Shernoff) The Haworth Press, Inc., 1997, pp. 59-72; and: *Gay Widowers: Life After the Death of a Partner* (ed: Michael Shernoff) The Harrington Park Press, an imprint of The Haworth Press, Inc., 1997, pp. 59-72. Single or multiple copies of this article are available for a fee from The Haworth Document Delivery Service [1-800-342-9678, 9:00 a.m. - 5:00 p.m. (EST). E-mail address: getinfo@haworth.com].

My mind spins in lockstep at a pace that scares me
The struggle to hold back tears again is lost
Thoughts of shared hugs come to mind
Words said in anger
Choices made for selfish pleasure
Regret

My God
"The pain then is part of the happiness now."
So the movie tells me
What of the lessons learned?
How can I be more?
I ask these questions through eyes blurred with tears again
I hold my face in my hands as I cry

I am sad
I am scared
I am not alone
Images of the past inform my present
Acknowledgment of blessings
Of passion then and now

The rhythm of life beats a challenging cadence
And so the task remains
Live on . . .

–Townsand Price-Spratlen, *Broken Silence, 1994*

FIRST THOUGHTS

I had just walked in the door of my apartment, and was greeted by the flashing red light of my message machine. The little leap of joy knowing that someone had called quickly turned to cautious stillness when I recognized her voice. It was unmistakable. She gently stumbled over my name with a kindness I had grown to enjoy. It was Tony's Mom. There was only one reason that she would call me; only one reason that she would leave a message on my machine. Tony had passed away, and she wanted to be sure that I knew as soon as possible. That was in September, 1994.

The week before Tony passed, I participated in the ADODI weekend retreat which was incredibly self-affirming and celebratory of love and the possibilities that faith creates. ADODI (pronounced "ah-DOE-dee") is a faith community of gay men of African descent with chapters in New York, Chicago and Philadelphia. We hold a retreat each summer so that folks can come together and share time, faith, learning, hurt, celebration, togetherness and the possibility of building tomorrow's tomorrow with strength and an affirming wholeness. The organization and the retreat are a living affirmation of the line by the late Essex Hemphill, "I guard my life with no apologies" (1986, p. 113). The guarding is self-affirming in act and in Spirit.

At the talent sharing during the retreat I read a poem that I wrote to Tony, but for some reason chose not to send to him. It spoke of the present as a bridge between the past and the future, and the truth that legacies made cannot be rewritten, but they can be redefined. I was given the gift of a caring ear of near-strangers, to listen to me and share in the mixture of love and desperation that I was feeling at the time. This combined three elements that have been, and continue to be, central to my ongoing transitions after Tony's passing: poetry, the spoken word, and an audience of near-unconditional acceptance. All three continue to play a key role in my ongoing efforts to "guard my life with no apologies," and celebrate the blessings of each new day.

As I stood there in the middle of the room listening to the voice of Tony's Mom, I began to trace time in the stunned silence of a moment I thought I had prepared myself for; reviewing past times I knew as intimacy, grasping desperately at the meaning of his sudden removal from this earth. Prepared? For what? I suddenly realized that I was not ready for the new challenge of being without Tony's presence on this side of life. The tears of sadness and fear began to fall at a pace I could not slow. I sat down to try to write, and no words came. The lines of a conversation Tony and I shared shortly after starting our relationship in 1991 played in my head over and over again.

"Do you believe in love at first sight?" I asked.

"Well, it depends on the sight, doesn't it?" Tony responded.

"True. The sight was you wearing that tight, ultra-white t-shirt and those sexy blue jeans with the strategic holes and bleach stains at the Brother-to-Brother meeting."

"You cruised me at a Brother-to-Brother meeting!?" Tony asked, honestly surprised.

"Of course I did. And so did several other pairs of eyes."

"Well then, ya. I guess I do believe."

Frantically, I searched for and quickly found "Broken Silence," the poem above which I had written seven months earlier, after speaking with Tony for the first time in weeks. Reading it again was my first step beyond those tears, a first step along a pathway of transformation that has brought me to now. A first step in my ongoing transformation of living beyond loss.

I had moved from the city we lived in just over a year before his death. A month prior to my move, Tony and I had agreed to end our love relationship, in order to remove the emotional and spiritual (and perhaps physical) strain of sustained romance while being thousands of miles apart. We did so knowing that the longing for each other would not end with a simple verbal agreement. We shared a hug, and from that moment forward I began embracing the distance between us. After listening to the message of his mother for the fifth time, I had seldom felt more guilty for having moved. While the move was "necessary" to make my next career step, careerist concerns suddenly sounded woefully hollow. In those moments, too many questions rushed to mind. Would it have made a difference if I had stayed? Perhaps not. Who will now take care of Smooch (Tony's dog whom he loved so much)? Can Smooch possibly understand that Tony will never again return to greet him at the porch steps? Can I? What do I call myself? What label now applies? We were never legally married, never even lived together, so how can I be a widower? Why am I attaching so much undo meaning to the significance a simple word provides? Will it give me the comfort I now seek?

I remain unsure of the answers to these questions, and, while troubling, the curiosity they provide is yet another of the many ambiguities in living my life after Tony's passing. I had lost a man who was once my lover, my partner, and whom I care for deeply. Amidst the ups and downs of building and sustaining our relationship, we shared the sweetest vulnerabilities that romantic love affords, celebrating each other in a life without veils, a life of fewer masks with each other. There is an unequaled void since his passing, having to learn to live a life without veils–and without Tony. It is a lesson I am learning still. While I may be blessed to share in this kind of love again, because of Tony, I know that expression of love can be real in my life, and for this knowledge, I am forever thankful.

MOVING WITH HIM STILL

Tony's passing has transformed my life by changing my view of, and relationship toward, expressions of faith and other spiritual celebrations. His passing teaches me that it is possible to live joyously, healthfully, and lovingly, and that any laughter shared is not disrespecting memories tinged with sadness. Such laughter is an expression of the diversity of emotional options that life provides, reminding me of the love passed that has been shared, and magnifying the value of prior moments in which I shared the same emotions with and without Tony when he was alive. We had enjoyed a relationship of queer desire, often relishing the gender-bending truths that were sometimes set in motion. These truths were of both behavioral and spiritual consequence, and were sometimes represented in the exchange of cards, gifts, and other symbols between us. Because of Tony, my feelings toward jewelry and other spiritual symbols have also changed. Tony's passing has made the meaning and method of "a balanced life" an everyday question, much more than something I am reminded of during a new December while making resolutions for the coming year.

Tony's death continues to transform my life in many ways, beginning with the reshaping of my thoughts about him. First, having faith that Tony would no longer have to suffer in the way that he did on this side was quite healing. This faith provides me with the reinforcement to embrace his release from discomfort, rather than viewing it purely in terms of life's loss. Second, there was the relief of a stress removed, of no longer having to anticipate a hurtful event. For us the living, all the anticipation of what may be that precedes the event itself was draining. As selfish as it may be, Tony's passing was, in a way, a burden removed. The late film maker Marlon Riggs' final words from *Tongues Untied* (1989) come to mind. ". . . and I am lightened, lifted, free . . ." Though he was talking about something else entirely, the phrase nonetheless has meaning here as well. Third, Tony's passing forced me to reach inside myself and feel feelings that I would just as soon funnel in a different, perhaps self-destructive way. Perhaps in the false images of a movie or the fiction of a good, sad novel. Or the emotional Novocain that alcohol provides. It has also led me to write things that are not the convenience of academic prose, nor the more comfortable expressions of keeping a journal.

Finally, his passing made me realize how much pride kept me from saying to him, from sharing with him. Already "too" emotional, pride prevented me from exhibiting any more emotion than necessary, whatever meaning I could give to that term. His passing, and the regrets that I try to hide, have helped heal me of the need to stand so substantially on a foundation of pride, and to instead stand on a foundation of shared concern, and expressed desire. Not to the point of disrespecting someone else's space, or being unnecessarily expressive, but just seeking the meaning of *honesty in the moment* that I'm living, far more often than I otherwise would have. The expression of that reduction of pride is reflected in the writing of this essay; a newfound willingness to process death and all its complexities. I no longer see death just as a limitation, an imposition of stolen moments; but also as an opportunity, as an element of every single moment that life and wellness exist; to share more deeply with those I'm fortunate enough to love. This is perhaps the greatest healing of Tony's passing; a freeing up to feel, to live, to be, and to be willing to experiment with the meaning, method and madness that lies within each of these truths.

Tony and I enjoyed a love, a gay love, that Tony's mother embraced, and my mother despised. That difference of maternal reactions always annoyed and embarrassed me. Tony's passing removed the embarrassment, no longer having to live out the difference through his eyes and magnified my annoyance, knowing that my Mom would likely never reach a place where she could embrace the man-love Tony and I knew as real. His passing is helping me to sometimes temper the value I place on my mother's view of my life and loves. Over time I have come to respect Tony's journey, as his passing helped educate me to the warrior metaphor as not just an

easy package to wrap a convenient set of victim-oriented perceptions in, but also as a part of the recognition that respect is seldom if
ever "complete." In other words, I could still respect and strive to
understand Tony, but at the same time, I didn't have to respect every
aspect of every choice of every moment that Tony co-created and
lived. Respect is about acknowledging complexity, and recognizing
that ambiguity in my response to the ongoing process as a whole, is
not a bad thing. It is in fact a good thing, a necessary thing. This
ongoing process leads me to seek simple refuge more often than I
should, and also prompts acts of random kindness, seeking out a
way to give back in the memory of someone who gave so much of
himself to me.

Because of a warm dependency that the miles between Tony and
I necessarily created after my move, Tony's passing has helped me
grow closer to my father. Dad represented me at Tony's memorial
service when time, distance, and the passing and funeral of another
family member just weeks before, prevented me from attending.
That dependency on my Dad to be at Tony's service in my stead,
along with his willingness to read my words at the gathering, far
from being a bad thing, was in fact, an act of fierce love that
continues to affirm our connectedness in many blessed ways.

LIVING THE SPIRIT, LIVING BEYOND LOSS

Beyond these thoughts about him, Tony's passing has transformed my life most profoundly by motivating me to refine and
celebrate a spiritual destiny. Because he was my lover, any spiritual
celebration I value could not be separated from our gayness, a
separation that might somehow minimize the love we shared. So I
continue seeking out a better understanding of spirituality and the
ways in which I can uncover and embrace my spiritual center. I
have had numerous conversations with others, asking them the
different ways in which they do so for themselves. Be it through
religious or institutional participation, introspective meditation, stu-
dying with teachers inspired by a higher source, or some other
strategy, I have long been curious about the means by which folks
come to an understanding of their spiritual selves. One such conversation with a friend in Philadelphia led me to ADODI.

ADODI is an organization of African American men who seek a meaning and method of being a man who loves men, linking gayness to its cultural, ideological and spiritual dimensions that go beyond the sex act, and focus instead on the process of affirming the different ways of love two men can share. Such a focus is recognized to be grounded in a spiritual identity, and the necessity then becomes specifying the rituals, tithes and other acts of faith that ground that identity in nurturing and affirming choices to help guide us from one day to the next. The annual summer weekend retreat is an important aspect of this process for me.

At the July, 1996 retreat during our first night together on Friday, we participated in a tribute to our ancestors, paying special recognition to those who have passed on before us. That ceremony helped galvanize for me the meaning of this year's retreat theme: Brotherhood of the Survivors. As gay men of African descent in late 20th century America, we are indeed a unique brotherhood, and the spiritual significance given to that term is largely shaped by how we understand the links that tie us one to another. After all, a brotherhood is defined as "an association of men united in a common interest, work, or creed" (Webster's Dictionary, 1968, p. 186). So the substance of the link defines the significance of the common unity we share. Not to the minimization of our differences, but instead affirming them while teaching ourselves how to "use each other's differences in our common battles for a liveable future" (Lorde, 1988, p. 74).

For me, the label "brotherhood of the survivors" is not focused solely on us the living. The label also includes all members of us past, present and future, since so many of the brothers who have now passed away laid the foundation upon which present and future expressions of the brotherhood will stand and grow. Thus the truths of our survival are perhaps best understood in a historical, as well as present focus, since it is the struggle to celebrate without shame our wholeness as gay men of African descent that is the link across the generations. Tony's passing has provided me with a strengthening motivation to seek out affirming ways to embrace and celebrate that wholeness, living each moment in the power and presence of a legacy which is left.

In other words, there is a thread of affirmation among the ties that bind us to each other, and by recognizing the present survivors, we are also recognizing the power of the legacy left in the many memories of the survivors who've gone before us, our ADODI IBAYE (deceased brothers). The ceremony that Friday night continues to have such an amazing power even as I write these words. It lifts up the possible and affirms my potential to seek out and realize those possibilities, sharing in the strength of a collective destiny that goes far back in history, and that is linked to the future, and the many men-loving men who will follow us in the years and decades to come. There were other aspects of the ceremony that also built on this theme of brotherhood, and the retreat as a whole was a realization of some of the many "possibility of possibilities" that Samuel R. Delany and the late Joseph Beam discussed in the seminal volume, *In the Life* (1986). I shared in the ceremony with Tony's memory fully on my mind, as oftentimes honesty in the moment demands strengthening the bridge between past hurt and present celebration.

The bottom line in all of this is that ADODI as an organization, and the retreat itself, is a celebration of spirituality through the sustenance and affirmation of a faith community. My faith extends, in part, from my search to give meaning to Tony's passing, and the power and beauty of men loving men upon which the love we shared was built. The faith that we of ADODI share in, need not be to a single God, the same God, nor any expression of a higher power necessarily. The faith is grounded in both the unseen power of a force greater than any person or being, AND in the lived experiences and realized possibilities that those of us in the brotherhood are creating with each new day we live. The focus of our faiths was as diverse as any other aspect of our multicultural selves (e.g., age, class background, skin tone, etc.). There were Buddhists, Agnostics, Baptists, Muslims, Catholics and many other religions which we practiced. Yet it was recognized that the strength of our brotherhood rests in part in our ability to build upon the strength within the "fund of necessary polarities," or multiple aspects of difference that Audre Lorde wrote of so eloquently (Lorde, 1984, p. 111). Our individual spirituality rests in part in some expression of collective participation, affirming some communal whole beyond our individual selves.

In addition to ADODI as an expression of my spiritual community, there are also many individual acts that are a part of my transformation beyond Tony's passing. I understand these individual
choices to be in a partnership with the collective choices that I
make. Just as a religious man finds celebration in the church, and
outside of the church in living out God's word, I, too, walk a similar
path. A few of these choices are considered below.

First, each day, shortly after awakening, and again shortly before
bed, I share a brief moment of prayer. These prayers most often
begin with the phrase, "Asante Sana, Amen-Ra for . . ." which
means thank you very much God. Amen-Ra was the God worshiped
by ancient Africans, a single name given to a God after the Africans
of the Lower Nile Valley who worshiped the God Amen, came
together with the Africans of the Upper Nile, worshipers of the
God, Ra, and called their God Amen-Ra. Calling His name helps
me remember that, like the ancient Africans, I, too, have differing
dimensions of myself that can be healthfully integrated into the
whole being I am striving to become.

These moments of prayer act to center me in the tasks of the
coming day, refining my priorities and the relationship between
my choices of this day, and the legacy of African greatness that
these choices are a part of. They remind me of the need to be
thankful for the many, many blessings I've been given, and am
being given with each new breath. These moments affirm the power
to create constructive change that lies within me and within us all,
and recognize that living out the duty to serve our people, and
grow in the midst of doing so extends the choices of destiny that
led so many other women and men of African descent toward
greatness.

Beyond these times near the beginning and ending of each day, I
stay in touch with my spiritual center by blessing the foods I eat
throughout the day. Doing so is a simple, quick reminder of eating
as a spiritual act, and a reminder that the food is an extension of a
continuum of effort that brought me to the moment in which I am
eating it. These moments of the blessing of the food are also a
reminder of the link between wellness, consumption and the power
of the blessing provided. Striving toward wellness, be it in movement and exercise, the eating of food, breathing deeply, or some

other choice, is also a spiritual act. These choices affirm realized possibilities in our struggle to challenge the many bigotries that are thrust our way as Lesbians and Gay men of African descent, and to find victory in the struggle itself, as well as in the spiritual embrace that any form of accomplishment provides.

Tony's passing helped me to discover a salient, spiritual presence in my life in adulthood for the first time. Because my parents almost wholly rejected their Southern, Baptist upbringing, I was reared in a household that was religious only in the most limited expressions of the term. We celebrated Christmas, and, as a small child growing up in Bellingham, WA, my parents involved the family in the Unitarian Church, perhaps the most liberal, non-rigid expression of Christian doctrine that exists. My parents created and maintained a household that was well versed in the "church of reason," as it has been called by others, where the intellect was celebrated on high, and the act of good grades in school was understood to be the only acceptable alternative. The extreme value placed on educational achievement was quite consistent with Southern, African American cultural doctrine. The nearly non-existent religious pretense was quite contrary to it. Tony's passing helped to move me beyond the church of reason alone, to a place where "desire and mourning and identity can interact in their full complexity" (Gates, 1993, p. 235), sometimes in the simplest choices.

For example, Tony's passing has brought the regular reading of fiction back into my life. At times when we were together, we would share fantasies, share desires for what might be, live out other possible lives, if only in our heads. Essentially we told each other stories, creating fiction off of the top of our heads. At times I recommended books of fiction to Tony that had touched me deeply, wanting to share the power of the creative word with him. With his passing, the importance of fiction has increased, to fill gaps in time that I might otherwise spend in needless grief, to remind myself that a part of the power of lost life lies in connections that cannot be touched, cannot be tasted, cannot be physically held. They are held within the mind and spirit, much like the resonance of a good story. Tony's passing has made that resonance all the more important.

Finally, music is a critical piece of my process of spiritual affirmation. Be it "religious" or secular, songs special to Tony and me, or those we never heard together, music provides me with an unyielding source of strength, warmth and the desire to move forward. Music was the reason for our first of many long conversations after we had known of each other for a few months (I had invited him to a Luther Vandross concert to which he was already planning to go with his mother). Music now serves as a reminder of the healing process that we shared on more than one occasion. Listening again to the songs that we heard together provides an auditory expression of the Spiritual echo that reinforces the truth that love sometimes provides. It is an echo that is a reminder of the sweetness that only acts of love make real. While sometimes little more than a hurtful reminder, these songs also remind me of the ever-present sharing that will forever mark Tony's presence in my life.

Intending no disrespect to a part of my ancestral legacy, I can't help but view the act of listening to music today in the light of the role that songs played in the Underground Railroad over a century-and-a-half ago. During that troubled time of chattel slavery, my ancestors used song lyrics to define a pathway toward freedom from the physical, psychological and spiritual bondage the masses of us were forced to endure. Today, while the stakes of freedom are thankfully quite different and less all-imposing (or so it seems), listening to music still provides a pathway toward a more humanized self, and a greater sense of joy. And it is this joy that music (and other cultural art forms) often provides which also rests at the core of my spiritual center. This morning it was Bebe and Cece Winans and Chante Moore that guided me from morning prayer through breakfast and final preparations before my bike ride to work. Yesterday morning it was Luther Vandross and Mahalia Jackson, and The Sounds of Blackness and Regina Belle guided me through the morning hours two days ago. I don't know whom it will be tomorrow. It really doesn't matter. I do know that it will be the voice of someone, celebrating notes of clarity and a purity of tone that lifts me up and sends me out the door ready to face an uncertain day with a very certain sense of the possible, and my ability to contribute to it in proactive and beneficial ways.

EMBRACING THE DISTANCE BETWEEN US

The outline that tracing time creates, like time itself, moves in one direction: forward. Yet, remembering past moments remains an important part of my ongoing process of, and effort toward, transformation. Remembering as a proactive choice, not trying to recreate a less hurtful truth, but rather to recognize the possible future with greater clarity. This emotional negotiation demands that I search to find a balance between grieving, acknowledging the enormity of losing Tony, and resisting the temptation to minimize at the same time, while not being immobilized by my reaction to his passing. The miles that were between us when he died magnified my fear that I was more of a hindrance to his well-being and his struggle to maintain it than I was a help. In order to transform the residue of guilt such concerns leave behind, I continue to evaluate the transition to being single again.

The transition from being a couple to being single again actually began prior to Tony's passing. As previously stated, a month before I moved and over a year prior to his death, we had come to a mutual agreement to build a friendship outside of a relationship, and to make that friendship as strong as possible. After having told that to someone who is also a Gay man of African descent, his reaction was, "Man, y'all must not've had much then. It must've been about nothin'." That is not true at all. A part of it was that we both realized that to try to maintain the relationship with geographic (and the potential for a growing emotional) distance between us as well, the pull for us both would likely not have been healthy.

The transformation to being single was also about trying to understand what being single is, what it means, and what it demands, including becoming more passionate about alone time, and prioritizing a holistic approach to a wellness lifestyle. This prioritizing galvanized a sense of purpose and a need to contribute to the world around me in new and untried ways. It was about normalizing the process of reaching out again, challenging the ease with which I sometimes forget the necessities of building—and sustaining—community.

As another piece of the paradox, I began this transition while in a new place, with a new job, in a different environment. Being in the midst of so many adjustments, the transformation to being single was another set of new things to contend with, in a rather long line of adjustments that I was already in the midst of. This helped me realize that moving on is not disrespectful. In fact, the moving on with consciousness of memory, and in celebration of legacies big and small, is a part of what I (perhaps naively) think Tony would actually want of me. The risk here is rationalization, but it's more than post hoc convenience. It's also a part of the duty attached to living well my next breath.

Finally, at one level the "transformation" beyond Tony's passing was and remains illusory. Trite as it may sound, Tony's physical presence on this side was in some ways the lesser of his manner of presence within the whole of my life. In the simplest of terms, he will always be with me, in that there is seldom a day that goes by that I don't think about him aloud, reflect on a moment we enjoyed, think about the special times we shared, and realize anew the enormous amount that he gave to me and my development, far beyond what I was able to acknowledge and share with him at the time. Tony was a man of joyous destiny, and embracing the transformation instigated by his passing is the least I can do to respect him while living beyond loss as best I can.

REFERENCES

Beam, J. (Ed.). (1986). *In the life: A black gay anthology.* Boston: Alyson Publications.

Gates, H. L., Jr. (1993). The black man's burden. In M. Warner (Ed.), *Fear of a Queer planet: Queer politics and social theory* (pp. 230-238). Minneapolis: University of Minnesota Press.

Guralnik, D. (Ed.). (1968). *Webster's new world dictionary of the American language.* Englewood Cliffs, NJ: Prentice-Hall.

Hemphill, E. (1986). Cordon negro. In J. Beam (Ed.), *In the life: A black gay anthology.* Boston: Alyson Publications.

Lorde, A. (1988). *A burst of light.* Ithaca, NY: Firebrand Books.

Lorde, A. (1984). *Sister outsider.* Freedom, CA: The Crossing Press.

Riggs, M. (Producer, Director). (1989). Tongues Untied [Film]. San Francisco, CA: News Reel.

The Merry Widower

Ron Najman

Remy died of AIDS a few hours after Christmas, 1994, in our house in Brooklyn. Had I known he was going to go that night I would have spent it with him, but instead I slept in a side room since the hospital bed left no space for a cot. The Russian woman who sat up with him woke me, saying she thought he had just passed. He wasn't breathing but was still warm. She asked if we should drape something over the mirror. I said it wouldn't be necessary. "Oh," she murmured, "English people do not do that." I asked to be alone. I fixed my gaze above Remy's body. "Go towards the light, Remy. The light, darling. You must not stay in this world. Go to the light. I love you."

Remy's mother Jeannine and brother Peter, and Peter's girlfriend Christine, had come from England one last time ten days earlier. We watched as the funeral home took his body down a deserted Wyckoff Street to be cremated. A mass was said three days later. The organist played "America the Beautiful," and the choir sang the sweet English national hymn "Jerusalem," to honor Remy's two countries. I read St. Paul's words about love that are often heard at weddings: ". . . Love suffers long and is kind; love envies not; love bears all things, believes all things, hopes all things, endures all things . . . ." Peter's words of appreciation focused on Remy's

Ron Najman is a publicist living in Brooklyn, New York. He was Media Director for the National Gay and Lesbian Task Force from 1984 until 1986.

[Haworth co-indexing entry note]: "The Merry Widower." Najman, Ron. Co-published simultaneously in *Journal of Gay & Lesbian Social Services* (The Haworth Press, Inc.) Vol. 7, No. 2, 1997, pp. 73-82; and: *Gay Widowers: Life After the Death of a Partner* (ed: Michael Shernoff) The Haworth Press, Inc., 1997, pp. 73-82; and: *Gay Widowers: Life After the Death of a Partner* (ed: Michael Shernoff) The Harrington Park Press, an imprint of The Haworth Press, Inc., 1997, pp. 73-82. Single or multiple copies of this article are available for a fee from The Haworth Document Delivery Service [1-800-342-9678, 9:00 a.m. - 5:00 p.m. (EST). E-mail address: getinfo@haworth.com].

power of seduction, an unusual theme for a church service, but an appropriate one if you knew Remy. For whether it was used to create a lover or a friend, seduction was Remy's defining gift. In his homily, Father Mark—who had visited Remy often in the last few months of his life—stood up to the forces of homophobia in his denomination and acknowledged that he had never seen a love stronger than that between Remy and Ron.

Then the dream began. It startled me at first, perhaps because I had rarely dreamt of Remy when he was alive. I was searching for something at our former house in Greenwich Village, aware that I didn't belong there. I was trespassing. Remy arrived, looking alive but being dead, appearing material but being immaterial, like Jesus standing before Thomas. We spent some time together, and then I insisted that he go to the spirit world, just as I had told him in our bedroom the night he died. You didn't have to be Anna Freud to figure this one out: My subconscious was trying to separate from Remy, and to fully accept his death. But in my waking reality I wasn't having much success doing that.

I knew I needed help when I realized that if I were to roll off the bed I would not fall down. I would be at almost the same level off the floor, supported by newspapers, magazines, junk mail, and empty takeout food cartons. No one ever said I was the neat one. Even at the office, without aggressive secretarial help my work area appears chaotic. (A security guard investigating a break-in once reported my desk had been "ransacked." "No," he was corrected. "That's normal.") Wanting to be left alone, I'd canceled the cleaning lady—a big mistake. Remy had known it would be difficult for me to keep the house tidy. He had told our friend Ina, "I don't know what Ron will do when I'm gone. You can't imagine how he was living when I found him."

I knew I was depressed and couldn't pull myself out of it. My physical health wasn't much better. I had spent the last several years out of shape, partly because of a bad reaction to a drug given for a resurgence of asthma, partly as a shield against temptation in the age of AIDS, and partly because I used food as a comfort. I had suspected Remy was infected as far back as 1983, and, except for occasional periods of denial, I'd carried a burden of silent sadness. Now that Remy was gone, I admitted I was damaging my health.

My blood pressure readings reflected it. Six months after Remy died I went to see my physician. Dr. Jim used the medical term: "Ron, you're a mess."

"I can obtain this kind of abuse from my friends, relatives and coworkers," I told him. "I don't need to pay you for it."

"Ron, what I mean is that your physical condition makes no sense because you could be moving on now, on to a wonderful new life. You've got a lot going for you. But you have to take care of your health."

I acknowledged that I agreed with him and that it was why, in part, I had come to see him. I wanted to get back into shape, to reclaim my health, to clean up my house, to get my life back on course, and to go look for happiness again. I just couldn't seem to do it.

I wasn't quite a basket case. During the winter following Remy's death I skied almost every weekend as I had done since childhood. But I was overweight, got winded easily, and felt the faint stirring of what might have been angina. And skiing was my only physical activity. I refused almost every offer to go out at night and people stopped calling. I had food delivered to the house. I read a great deal, mostly about my political philosophy, libertarianism, and watched *The X-Files* on television on Fridays. I saw almost none of our friends. By summer I was going to bed long before it was dark out, and sleeping as late as possible, twelve hours a day or more.

"I've been keeping the exterior of my house neat, clean, swept of leaves and shoveled of snow," I told my doctor. "Inside, it's festering. I haven't picked up anything I dropped unless it was on fire. My friend Susan passed by with her little daughter, knowing that the back garden must be in full bloom. 'It is', I told her, 'but I can't let you bring Claire through the house. A child shouldn't see a grown-up living like this. It will scar.' "

"Why do you think moving on is so hard for you?" Jim asked. "Remy and I were supposed to go through eternity together," I told him. "Yet I can't see myself being happy again unless I have another man in my life. It feels like a betrayal. I don't know what to do. Frankly, I don't want to start getting back into shape yet because people will know it means I'm looking for someone new and conclude that I'm being disrespectful to Remy. They'll say that my hair is turning gold with grief, that I'm acting like the merry widower."

"Ron, you're getting in the way of your own recovery. See somebody about this, now."

I went home and thought about it. In recent years, friends had lost husbands or lovers to cancer, heart attacks, and, of course, AIDS, so I didn't feel singled out by life. But I did feel hurt by it. At a dinner gathering, a widow joked with me that if our spouses were still alive, we could see ourselves having an affair, but with them dead it was simply out of the question. Was this the way it would be for the rest of my life?

I made an appointment with a therapist. Joan was a social worker, gay-lesbian affirming, and had experience with bereavement. She quizzed me about my years with Remy. I didn't want to talk about things that hurt. I felt guilty over the times I had been too hard on him, or too moody, or insensitive to his needs. I wanted to remember the good times we spent with friends and family, or watching Benny Hill and Britcoms on TV, or coming home from a day's skiing to a meal he had prepared for us. I wanted to mourn him just by thinking about how very much I loved him. "You must mourn the whole person," Joan said, "not an idealized version of him. And you must deal with your life as it really happened, both the good and the bad."

She told me about a middle aged woman, stylish and active when her mother died, who couldn't let go. Slowly, she adopted her mother's manners, attitudes, and aging outlook on life. She began wearing her mother's frumpy clothes. She moved into her mother's house. She became her mother, and gave up her own life in the process.

Our relationship had had what I suspect are the ordinary growing pains common to many gay male couples. Over the years we learned to communicate better, but there were some outstanding issues. Undoubtedly, Joan sensed that I harbored a few disappointments over our life together. I started talking to her about them.

Remy was one of the kindest men you could ever have hoped to meet. He was generous with his time, loved being with people of all ages and all descriptions, and always expected the best in others. He was well-educated, wonderfully fit, utterly charming, and had a commanding voice and a marvelous Oxonian accent. At first meeting, most people found him fascinating.

He was also a dreamer and lacked practicality, especially in the area of finances. His income was sporadic, and, generally speaking, his attitude towards social conventions reminded me a little bit of a phrase from Herb Gardner's play *A Thousand Clowns*: "slightly to the left of whoopee." Our rent-controlled apartment was so inexpensive that I didn't much mind covering the bills when his writing projects didn't pan out, but I tired of that, and he realized he wasn't being fair to me. He eventually worked very hard at two successive businesses, but they failed, and at his death he left me with expenses and no insurance.

Another area I discussed with Joan was sex. Neither of us was possessive, or particularly bothered by the thought of the other in bed with another man. There was only one negative incident involving a third party, and it was resolved with Remy and I achieving a better understanding of each other. By the standards of New York at the time, we were not very promiscuous.

AIDS hit ten years into our time together. To be as safe as possible we decided to have a sexually exclusive relationship, and most of the time were able to abide by this agreement. We also started practicing safe sex with each other, and although these changes probably saved my life (I'm HIV negative), they came too late to save Remy. But even when our relationship was open I had been more conservative philosophically than he was when it came to sex on the side. I had grown even more so as the AIDS epidemic progressed, and as I'd thought about the effects of promiscuity on society. I knew intellectually that I could have been the one who contracted AIDS but I felt a certain distress thinking that if Remy had just been a bit more conventional in his views, or more cautious in his behavior, maybe we would have been spared this misery.

I found myself brooding over Remy's stiff-upper-lip aloofness. He'd rarely express any sentiment about our union, and I'd chalked this up to English boarding school reserve. But how many times can a lover forget your birthday and expect not to be the object of a murder contract? He'd gotten better as he got older, yet I found myself thinking of little things he had done (or not done) that had hurt a bit or had made me feel slighted. I started questioning how much Remy had loved me and how much I had loved him.

This was not what I had expected to encounter in the mourning process. I knew the books said that one of the stages of mourning is anger, and my Aunt Rose had warned me about it. But I wasn't just angry; I was obsessing over past disappointments. Rage was building in me. Sometimes life was the target, and sometimes it was just Remy. I started wondering if I had done the right thing by being his lover. If only I'd left him over the money issue or some other dispute, maybe I would have found someone else, someone who wouldn't have gotten AIDS, someone who wouldn't have died and left me alone.

These doubts seemed crazy to me. Despite the rough spots, Remy and I had been happy together. We'd had our bouts of dysfunctionalism and co-dependency, but we'd lasted 21 years. So why were these things troubling me, now that he was gone?

And something else seemed odd to me. I didn't cry for Remy after he died. I'd cried through the entire night the day he was officially diagnosed with a dangerously low T-cell blood count, a little the next night, and then no more. I remember thinking I mustn't cry, I must steel myself for the road ahead; if I go to pieces, I won't be any use to him during his ordeal.

Joan suggested that even in the best of relationships—and she didn't doubt that Remy and I had had a good one—there are disappointments and tensions. As long as your partner is there with you, you are getting something in return—love, emotional support, companionship—that makes the deficits seem unimportant. When your lover dies you no longer receive the positive reinforcement, and the deficits can stand out in your memory. That was what was happening to me. I accepted that, but I knew there was something else going on. Something greater was driving my anger towards life and clouding my thoughts of Remy, something I just couldn't access, or didn't want to face. A seemingly unrelated event held a key.

Several months into my bereavement therapy I learned that someone I had known had overdosed on drugs, and that her death might have resulted from feelings brought on by sexual childhood abuse. When I was growing up, an older child in the neighborhood had physically abused me. There was a small amount of sexual abuse as well, not purposefully sexual, just an extension of the physical taunting.

I had long ago convinced myself it wasn't important. I hadn't had a very happy childhood, but then, a lot of people don't. In my twenties, I'd seen a psychiatrist for a few years, and then a psychologist. They helped me with some issues, but I never thought that dredging up the past should be a lifelong preoccupation. It's important to know what made you the person you are today, but having achieved that understanding, it's time to get on with your life. Still, I felt I should explore this abuse business now.

I started talking about it to Joan and to others. I read a couple of books on child abuse and learned that it leaves the victim feeling betrayed and abandoned, and that those who have gone through incest or sexual abuse often have problems with sex and self-image. Mike Lew, in his book on male abuse survivors, *Victims No Longer*, writes: "An incestuous childhood shatters the survivor's self-esteem and causes him to be left with an unrealistic picture of himself. . . . He feels ugly and unlovable." Many in this field believe that it doesn't take years of overt sexual abuse to damage a child's confidence and self-esteem: a single act of abuse can do it. I realized that I'd never gotten over my abuse. I admitted to myself that I had felt abandoned by my parents for their failure to prevent it. (In their defense, they never knew it happened. They're wonderful people and I love them.)

Getting honest about that part of my past led me to talk to Joan about something else I'd repressed, the fact that most of my life I've had a fear of being on my own. Not of being physically alone–I often go skiing or do other things by myself and enjoy it–but of being without someone to count on emotionally. When I was born my mother went through postpartum depression. That had come out the last time I'd seen a shrink, almost thirty years ago. It's likely that my mom's problem left her emotionally unavailable to me as an infant. I remembered how, when deposited at my grandparents' house as a youngster, I would stand by the window for hours watching for my parents to return in their Studebaker.

I admitted to myself that Remy's death had stirred up my childhood fears of being abandoned, of being alone, an old hurt I'd never put to rest. And some serious problems with self-esteem. Here I was, widowered, close to 50 years old, out of shape, and wondering if I was ever going to find another lover. I was feeling unlovable and abandoned, much as I'd felt as a child (especially when being mistreated). I was angry at Remy for leaving me in this situation as an adult. And that is why it was so hard for me even to think of getting my life together and looking for another man. I did not want to abandon Remy the way I felt others had abandoned me.

Remy had been my defense against the distress of my childhood. He was charming and liked by everyone, and being his lover made up for the doubts I had about my personal worth (his pet name for me was "Handsome"). He would be kind to me and love me, and make up for the bad things done to me as a child. We would grow old together, die within a few years of each other, and eventually be together in heaven, where the emotional security would continue. But Remy died much too soon, not when we were, in Yeats's words, "old and grey and full of sleep." I still had decades of life ahead of me.

It wasn't until I brought half of Remy's ashes to England for burial in the garden of Peter's vineyard that I finally broke down. I planted two small rosebushes–bright red, Remy's favorite color, one for him, one for me–and cried deeply into the English soil.

I'm able to express my emotions, sure. But letting myself feel the emotions in the first place is a different story. If something hurts badly enough, I put it out of my mind. I put it someplace where it causes trouble later. That's what I did with the pain of the abuse I went through as a child. And that's what I did in my mourning process. That was why I couldn't get in touch with the anger I felt at Remy for leaving me until more than a year after his death. And that was why I couldn't cry over Remy's death for so long.

If I'd been able to cry earlier, if I'd let the feelings out, I probably would not have sunk into the depression that led me to go see my physician. Instead, I had tried to tough it out. I did the same stiff-upper-lip routine that I had charged Remy with.

Joan helped me through the mourning process. I'm close to its end. I'm getting back into shape, and I am dating. Or, as I occasionally put it to friends, holding auditions. While I haven't cast the new male lead yet, I've met some great men. It's nice to know they're still out there. The first man I had sex with after Remy died helped bring me back to feeling fully alive.

I always believed that if you have enough faith, the right things, the good things, happen to you. It's just that it's hard to keep faith, especially when you're challenged by a devastating emotional event like the loss of a spouse. Still, that's when you need faith the most. So I decided to open myself up to the beneficence of the universe, and, just as I'd hoped, I started meeting guys. And I'm grateful. Faith, it is said, is half dependent on gratitude. The other half is patience, which is for me the hard part.

I've gotten my life back under control, and my house cleaned up (I'm even doing a long-needed renovation). Remy would have been pleased. Most importantly, I'm healing on several levels, including the spiritual one.

As for that incomprehensible question as to why Remy had to die, I can only posit the following. I believe that we do live forever, for a time in this world and for a time in the world we cannot see. Remy and I will be reunited someday, in a different form in a different place. If I find a new lover, he will be with us as well, for all the people we have known and loved and who have known and loved us will be there. The egoism, possessiveness, and hurts of our earthly lives are an illusion, and do not exist in the next world, which is our real home. Love is the only thing that is real, the only thing that endures.

Why did Remy have to leave me? I think we are here to learn lessons. This world is a classroom, a laboratory. I think God wanted me to be alone for a while, to deal with the sadness and emptiness and to work on building a stronger spirit. I've made some progress.

Remy's charming, happy-go-lucky nature made people want to be around him. But he was unhappy at the end of his life that he had never been financially successful, and that he hadn't been as attentive to our relationship as he might have been (the same charge to which I plead guilty). He learned that actions do have consequences, that if you don't prepare for the future and tend to the details in life there will be regrets. Having learned that, it was time for him to go.

After I emerged from hibernation, I asked friends and family whether they thought Remy had loved me, and whether it appeared

I had loved him. I needed to ask them this to deal with my turmoil. They were astonished by the question, because it was so obvious, they said, that we'd been devoted to each other. Christine told me she moved in with Peter only after visiting our home in America: "Seeing you loving each other changed my life." The doubts I had after Remy's death were no more than ghosts from the past, and now they're gone. Ultimately, the love Remy and I had for each other was proven unconditional.

Remy was skeptical about spiritual matters and doubted whether there was anything beyond this life. I told him it didn't matter, that there was another world and we would all be in it, whether he thought so or not.

There is a story in Remy's family of his grandmother seeing a medium after the death of her second husband, Tommy, a charming inventor and noted party animal. Grandmother just wanted to see if Tommy was all right. The medium reported that Tommy said, "Everything's fine here. It's like one long cocktail party." That truly would have been Tommy's idea of heaven, Remy had told me. He knew I treasured that story, and I figured he might just try to make contact. He did.

For several days after his death, until well after the funeral mass, I heard Remy's voice—not his earthly voice, more like a telepathic communication. In his clearest message he said to me, "Don't worry Ron. I'm here, and everything's fine. It really is. Oh, and you were right about heaven."

Good, because I hate being wrong about anything. Love is real. Over in England, I'm told those rosebushes are growing towards each other.

A Dream Is More Than a Wish Your Heart Makes

Jon L. Clayborne

Several weeks before Steve died I began to have a recurring dream in which Steve and I were dressed in running shorts and tank tops as we jogged along in a dark void. At first, we kept up pace with each other, taking each stride at ease. After a while, Steve began to fall behind me. He was still running without straining, but he couldn't keep up with me. Each time I looked back, I could see the distance between us growing wider and wider, and Steve's image getting smaller and smaller. Steve could see the look on my face imploring him to run faster and catch up with me, but all he could do was to look back hopelessly as if to say "I'm doing the best I can." Somehow we both realized that I couldn't stop and wait for him, let alone turn back.

Where it had begun as a dream, I began envisioning the same images in my waking hours, too. Two figures in a black void. Sometimes it took a moment or two before Steve was trailing behind me; other times the distance between us was already established and continued to increase at a more rapid pace. When I looked behind me Steve was still in sight, but I knew as his image grew smaller and smaller sooner or later he would disappear. I was

Jon Clayborne lives happily in New York City with his significant other, Doug and their cat, Alexis. He can be reached vie e-mail at: dougjon@msn.com.

[Haworth co-indexing entry note]: "A Dream Is More Than a Wish Your Heart Makes." Clayborne, Jon L.. Co-published simultaneously in *Journal of Gay & Lesbian Social Services* (The Haworth Press, Inc.) Vol. 7, No. 2, 1997, pp. 83-99; and: *Gay Widowers: Life After the Death of a Partner* (ed: Michael Shernoff) The Haworth Press, Inc., 1997, pp. 83-99; and: *Gay Widowers: Life After the Death of a Partner* (ed: Michael Shernoff) The Harrington Park Press, an imprint of The Haworth Press, Inc., 1997, pp. 83-99. Single or multiple copies of this article are available for a fee from The Haworth Document Delivery Service [1-800-342-9678, 9:00 a.m. - 5:00 p.m. (EST). E-mail address: getinfo@haworth.com].

never one to search for meanings in dreams, but this one was so in my face, so obvious. In the Summer of 1992, Steve was very ill; his attending physician had diagnosed chronic cirrhosis of the liver. Halfway through his three-month hospitalization in St. Vincent's Hospital the doctor advised me that Steve's condition was terminal. Maybe within months, certainly no more than a year, my lover would be dead.

It turned out to be a couple of months; the length of one Summer. A few days after Labor Day, in the early morning of September 10th, I was awakened by the telephone ringing at my bedside. As soon as I heard the doctor's voice all I could say was, "Oh no. Not my baby!" Immediately, I took hold of myself and faced up to reason. I knew it was going to happen. I knew it would be soon. In fact, Steve had had a pretty bad week, so bad that only a couple of days earlier his father and I had to drive him from his folks' place in Brooklyn into Manhattan late at night to have him re-admitted to St. Vincent's.

This was the first time in thirteen years that I was not half of a couple; the second time in twenty-two that my relationship with another man had ended. Half my life had been spent living with and loving another man. My daily routine had come to depend on me interacting with another person, with my lover. My heart, the center of my being, had been wrenched out of my body. Alone, what was I going to do? I suppose, if I had become absorbed about my future at the beginning I might have become paralyzed by doubts and the anguish. Thankfully, there were things that had to be done, regardless if I thought I was ready or not. There were some immediate things of concern, like what was I going to do with an apartment that while affordable for two was beyond my means to rent alone.

Then there was work. I was stagnating in my job. Now that I had no obligations to anyone but myself I could do some career planning. Not only could I focus on looking for a new job, I could widen my search to another city, another country even. There was so much for me to consider all at once I didn't know where to start. So I didn't start; not right off. Instead, I resumed my daily routine pretty much as it had been before hospital visits and late nights had disrupted it. I had my coffee before rushing off to work in the morning. I made it myself, but I did have it. Some evenings I'd head for the gym after work, other nights I'd stay at home reading or watching the television. There seemed little change from what I had been doing for years; however, everything I did felt peculiar for a while. There was never any question in my mind that I would go on. I just had to go on by myself. I had to learn to define myself in the singular.

As part of a couple, there were times when I'd really enjoyed being separate every now and then. Whether going to the gym or going off somewhere else in private for a couple of hours or so, I didn't mind doing some things by myself. Now forced to do every-thing on my own, I felt alone a lot of the time. I didn't feel alone because there was no one sitting on the sofa watching the television with me, or when I ate out, because I often ate by myself. I felt alone, because I was missing a part of me; something that had given me balance for so many years. I could be in a crowded office, or amid a joyous group at a party when I would get the sensation of being isolated from everyone else. Perhaps there had been some other time in my life when I felt this alone, but it must have been a long time ago. I had no recollection of ever feeling so desolate.

Nor was it that I didn't feel loved, because I knew I was. I expected friends to be supportive, and they were very supportive. The one thing that would have made the situation better was beyond human capacity to do. The next best thing was making sure that I was loved, and my friends did that. To have one friend that so unselfishly took my welfare to heart would have been good fortune; I had two. Tony and Debra. Tony saw to it that I was not alone most weekends, especially after Steve died. Although Tony had moved to Edison, New Jersey, he'd come into Manhattan to stay at my apart-ment, or else he got me to board Amtrak for the half-hour trip to his new house. We'd make plans to go to the movies, or hit a bar, but more than usual we'd just go to sleep after a late dinner or shopping in the malls (the "Malling of New Jersey" we'd call it).

By the beginning of 1993, it had been over a year since I had a vacation; the last time being when Steve, Tony and I had gone to Palm Springs. I probably would have gone on without thinking about the need to get away; however, Tony broke the inertia by proposing that the two of us head to Florida–a few days in SoBe and a few days in Key West. He turned it over to me to make the hotel and flight bookings, things I'd always let Steve handle in the past. Before I'd met Steve, I had never really thought about taking vacations to resorts or any distant destination, other than to visit friends or family. We'd been together less than a year when Steve decided we should take a holiday in Puerto Rico; without my involvement, he had the flights booked and the hotel reservations made. Thereon Steve took care of all our travel plans, only consulting me to find out if I could clear the dates he'd chosen with my boss. I realized there was no magic or expertise involved in making travel arrangements, but it was always part of Steve's domain. On my own again, I was not going to stop taking vacations. Nor could I wait for someone else to come along to make plans.

I called the travel agent Steve had always used. After first relaying the news about Steve, and getting condolences, I proceeded to make arrangements for the flight and lodging in Miami. I sent away for several brochures for guest houses in Key West. After Tony and I went through them and made a decision, I called to arrange for the second leg of our stay in the Keys. I even rented a car. For years I had been making most of my business travel plans, choosing flights, dialing Hertz, and occasionally finding a hotel room. Strangely, I had never had to do this for my personal enjoyment; it felt like a real accomplishment to make vacation arrangements on my own. I kept busy with Tony and other friends, Darryl, Charles and Colin, Andy, and Jimmy; and of course, there was that job to go to during the work week. Still there were many times when I felt I was all alone. It took time to work my way through this feeling, but I knew I had to be patient; as unpleasant as those moments seemed, they passed eventually. I don't mean for it to sound that I was callous to my emotions, or that I had found some miracle path to closure that sidetracked the natural feelings of hurt when someone you love dies. I had my periods of crying and feeling sorry for myself.

Most of the guys I know who have been in relationships that ended could put the blame on another man, career goals, boredom, or different growth patterns; most of them did not have their lovers die. And when a lover had died, the death all too frequently had resulted from complications arising from AIDS, not something so mainstream as alcoholism. I found it bizarre that a lover of mine could have died from booze. What kind of odds were at play here? I couldn't win the lottery, but I could have a lover die from cirrhosis of the liver! Not only was it unfair, it was stupid. Too stupid to have happened to me. On the other hand, there were times when I could be so objective in evaluating what had happened that I'd become detached from the situation and feel that it was someone else's experience. Sometimes, I'd drift off into a conversation with myself:

Self A: How do you feel about being alone.

Self B: I'm not really alone, I've got friends, family.

Self A: And when they're not around!

Self B: I keep myself busy.

Self A: Doing what?

Self B: The usual. Work, the gym, day-to-day stuff.

Self A: And when you're not at work or the gym. What about at home? In the evening?

Self B: I guess I find something to do to keep myself busy. I watch TV. I read. Think. Whatever! I find something to do until it's time to go to bed.

Self A: This keeps you from feeling lonely?

Self B: Sometimes.

Self A: So there are times you do feel lonely?

Self B: I guess.

The conversation would end, and I'd think, "Poor guy; he's having such difficulty admitting that he is lonely."

I wasn't so detached from reality that I didn't realize that it was me who was feeling so desolate that I didn't want to admit how lonely I felt. I never told anyone how bad I felt, nor did anyone ask me specifically. A couple of people suggested that I attend a bereavement group. I appreciated the concern, but I never felt I needed to sit down with others to move on through the stages of grieving. There was nothing at all wrong with it, and if I had needed it I have no doubt that I would have sought out and joined a group. I just didn't feel that it was necessary for me. As bad as I felt, I accepted the loneliness as part of the process I'd work through. I do tend to keep my deliberations to myself; nonetheless, I do a lot of thinking. I've always thought of myself as being a stoic; I can accept the reality of a situation and move on without too much emotion. I automatically took this approach to handling my transition through this grief.

Another part of the process was observing the "anniversaries"; more correctly identified as the "firsts." They could have been any moment that occurred within the first year of Steve's death, and were most noticeable during traditional observances. During those twelve months I silently observed a string of firsts. His birthday fell in early October, so not long after he died it was his first birthday since his death. The next month was the first Thanksgiving following his death. In succession came the first Christmas, the first New Year, my first birthday, the first vacation, the first Spring, the first Summer, and ultimately the real first anniversary of Steve's death. And, in between were all the little firsts. The first day back in the office; the first evening coming home from work; the first weekend; the first time eating out. I was so aware of them at the time.

I became aware of the anniversaries the day after Steve's death. I'd been living in our apartment by myself for three months. Before his terminal diagnosis, we'd assumed that Steve would return; even after his condition looked so dire I thought about making arrangements to take care of him when he came home. By the time Steve decided that he wanted to be released to his parents' care I realized that he would never be back in our apartment. Still, as long as he was alive, it was our home.

One of the first thoughts I had when I awoke the morning after Steve died was that he could never come back to the apartment. No matter how unlikely, as long as he had been alive he could have returned, somehow. Now, even the most extreme possibility of his coming home ended with his death. He'd never, ever walk through the front door again. He'd never feel sunshine on his skin; never feel a breeze blow across his cheek. I'm sure I started to cry with each thought. By the time I awoke the next morning, I thought, a whole day would have passed that Steve could no longer experience. The first day that he would not know since his birth. The day following Steve's death was a sorrowful "first," but the days leading up to his birthday were the worst. Coming in October, it was not long after Steve had died. If he'd lived just less than a month longer, he would have turned forty-four. As short as the time was until his birthday, it still gave me twenty-odd days to dread its arrival.

Birthdays are more special to me than any other annual observance. It's a day set aside to demonstrate your gratitude to someone you love for their being a part of your life, and vice versa. It's a gift-giving celebration like Christmas, but the focus is on one person. A lover's birthday is not to be forgotten or overlooked. More than another day to say "I love you," a birthday is an occasion to show him how much he means to you in whatever way you choose. A card. A dinner. A gift. Routine, made gratifying by thoughtfulness and adoration. I dreaded the arrival of Steve's birthday in that brief period leading up to it after his death. I expected the day to be the most painful I'd experience. It would be made notable not only by his absence, but by the absence of cards and telephone calls of good wishes. I'd cross off each day on a mental calendar, feeling more anxious as his birthday got closer. After all my concern, the actual birthday was anti-climactic. As I'd projected, I was very aware of the day. No birthday greetings appeared in the mailbox. Not a telephone call. No restaurant reservations. No gift secretly wrapped and hiding in the bedroom closet under a pile of sweaters. Everything that hadn't happened or wasn't done reminded me that it was Steve's birthday; yet, I didn't feel any sadder than I had for the preceding month. I had been dreading the day for so long that when it arrived it could not fulfill the anticipation.

I don't think I pondered or became anxious over any of the other "firsts"; they occurred with little or no apprehension. Inexplicably, sometimes these milestones would cause tears to well up, other times they would make me smile at the memory, and sometimes they would not have any effect on me. I convinced myself that I was unemotional, but more accurately I just didn't like giving way to public demonstrations of my grief. I accepted that it would take some indeterminate time to work through the grief. In many ways grieving was simple compared to knowing what I should do next to re-start my life. My life had been totally upended for months. I had accepted that my life had changed, but I didn't think about the change in me. I foresaw some kind of natural progression moving me onto a new stage of life; however, I was content to passively stand aside, letting whatever happened determine my direction and next move. Aside from periods of sorrow and occasional feelings of being alone, I was resigned to getting on with my life.

Tony and Debra both had been telling me that I had to start paying some attention to myself during Steve's illness. I was quick to respond that there would be plenty of time for me to devote myself to my welfare later. When the time came that I no longer had Steve as an excuse, I did virtually nothing to take control of my life again. The first several months it was just enough to get back to a more regular routine. No more hospital visits, no more nighttime workouts, no more late evening diner meals by myself. I don't remember spending any weekends alone during that time; as I mentioned, Tony saw to it that we got together in the City or out in Jersey at his new house. I kept busy, doing most of the things I'd been doing for years. This routine lasted for close to a year. Life had become like a karaoke machine. The strings, the horns, the drum, the rhythm were all there; everything but a unique voice to give it style. What vocals there were, were weak and repetitive.

As my friends had said, I had to start paying attention to me, not only my day-to-day needs but my desires and hopes. To tell the truth, while I had resolved to continue living I had done little more than make sure that I would breathe in and out every few seconds. I went through so many different moods in a year's time. Yes, the sorrow and sadness of no longer being able to see someone I had loved so deeply. Not surprisingly there was a lot of anger. I was mad with Steve for not letting me know how sick he was. I was convinced that he had decided long before he knew he was ill that he would die at a young age. Indeed, he had told me as much in the hospital. He had never thought he would live to be 45. He died before his forty-fourth birthday. My anger mixed with hurt the more certain I felt that Steve had chosen to let life slip away without a struggle. I began to wonder how much of what I saw as his conscious decision was a rejection of our relationship. I began to question the substance of the thirteen years I'd spent with this one man.

Out of this sense of anger and uncertainty, I resolved that I had become too subservient. It hadn't solidified my relationship with Steve; and it may well have contributed to its demise. On my own again, it was time to do what I wanted to do for me. Following months of cruising along I wanted to take control of my life, to determine what I wanted for myself. For a brief moment, I thought that I would never allow myself to fall in love again. I thought to myself that, yes, I'd been able to bury one lover; yet even if I could go through that kind of pain again I didn't want to. Who would! Equally of concern, did I ever want anyone to go through what I had suffered? How could I cause anyone I love that much pain. I'd had two long-term relationships. Why not consider myself fortunate to have had two lovers in my life. Closing in on middle age, I could certainly find a life for myself by myself. For a brief moment, I really did think that I could proceed through the rest of my life without being opened to the possibility of falling in love again.

Ironically, the same dread that had caused me to reject the possibility of falling in love again convinced me that I should not close any doors. I'd been able to move on in other areas of my life, although it was difficult. There were places I avoided for a long time because the memories were too upsetting. During warm weather, on nice evenings, Steve would often be waiting out on the street corner by our building. About half a block away he'd recognize me walking from the subway. He'd begin to wave joyously. Before I moved to a new apartment following his death, frequently I'd have the unsettling experience of walking home and envisioning Steve eagerly waiting for me on the same corner, waving. Until very recently, I wouldn't walk near the block where we had lived. Even now, there are CDs I am reluctant to play because I associate them with Steve; especially music he listened to during his hospitalization.

Memories that have been brought up in writing this essay have made me stop from time to time to recompose myself. Regardless of the hurt there comes the realization that my grief gave evidence to my ability to love, to fall in love. Regardless of any uncertainties I had about my relationship with Steve, there was no denying that love had existed between us; looking back I could say I had loved. I wasn't about to deprive myself of so much happiness even at the risk of losing it again. Of course, whether or not someone came along was something else. My first relationship lasted ten years, followed by my thirteen years with Steve. After twenty-three years of not only not being out there, but never having been there, how do you begin to play the field? Without frequenting bars or spending much time cruising, I'd been fortunate to have had two lovers by my mid-forties. While I didn't rule out the possibility of settling down again, I didn't see it as very likely. Besides, the idea of dating took my fancy. More than ever, I now had the chance to meet a nice guy anywhere, at any time; maybe at the gym, or in the office, or grocery shopping, or through friends. I could go out for a meal with some guy, take in a movie or a show. If we enjoyed each other's company we could move on to another level; however, it would be clear that no promises were being exchanged. We'd be free to date someone else the next night, whether or not we decided to see each other again.

Never having had the chance to live alone as an adult, I welcomed the experience to develop a sense of who I was on my own. I had never been shy about my political opinions in public, yet I'd taken a backseat in my personal relationships. In order to re-start my life after Steve's death, I had to decide on a lot of things for myself, all by myself. Where did I want to live? How did I want to decorate my apartment? What movie did I want to see? Whether to eat in or go out. Whether to remain in New York. Relocating became a major consideration. At first I approached the idea of moving with a sense of whimsy. I delighted in the realization that I could move anywhere I wanted; across town; across the continent; across the world.

Decades of travel had taken me to several cities that I had thought I could easily call home: Boston, San Francisco, Toronto, Frankfurt, and London. Any thought of re-locating in the past had never gone beyond conjecture. Family or lovers had always kept me in New York. Suddenly after twenty-five years, I felt like an orphan and a widow. My parents were deceased, and I had no lover. On top of the turmoil in my personal life I was burned out at work. I wasn't looking to run away and to forget the trauma of the past several months, I wanted to find a place and a situation where I could resume my professional and personal development. I needed renewal and a physical move seemed to hold that promise.

I flew out to San Francisco that November with two objectives. One, after three years this trip had become a tradition; Steve and I would get together with Debra and Paula for Thanksgiving week, culminating in a huge feast for about two dozen in Debra's apartment on the Thursday. This time I'd be by myself. What would it be like to go places and do things I had previously done always with Steve? The second was exploring the possibility that I might move West. I didn't find a job on that visit to San Francisco, or any subsequent visit although I made an effort to contact some leads once I was back in New York. In hindsight, I should have just picked up and moved; but I didn't feel that secure that I could relocate without some means of support. One thing I did do seems fairly inconsequential, but at the time it was very important to me. I got my ear pierced.

I'd been intrigued with the idea of getting my ear pierced for years. All I ever had in mind was something simple, something small, fairly discreet. What few times I'd voice interest in getting an earring in the past I'd had to defer to Steve's none so subtle aversions. I suppose if I had felt very strongly about it I would have done it despite Steve's objections, but while it always remained an appealing thought I didn't make it an issue. Like most things, I was willing to concede. Somehow the earring became an obsession on this trip. I wanted to do it, but now I had my own doubts. How would it go over at work? Then again, did I really care what anyone at work thought about it. Eventually, I could take it out during the day, but a stud would have to stay in continuously for at least six weeks once I got back to New York in order for the hole to stay open. Well, I was only planning on wearing a small stud most of the time anyway, though I might put a hoop in on special occasions. Within a few minutes of rushing up the steps of The Gauntlet, my ear was pierced and a tiny gold stud had been inserted through the opening. Looking at it in a hand mirror, my first thought was, I did this on the advice of some flight attendant I met in a gym? Then I smiled. No, way! I got the earring because I wanted it. And I loved it. It was one of the first concrete things I did that showed I was taking what I wanted into consideration. I really could do something for myself, and myself alone.

I returned to NYC giddy and enthusiastic; and ready for a trip to London–this time on business. As with San Francisco, London posed an emotional challenge. I'd made my first trip to the UK a year earlier. Steve had felt very dejected because he could not accompany me on my first overseas business trip. At that time, we'd just gotten back from Thanksgiving in San Francisco, and earlier in the year we'd been to Palm Springs. We didn't have the funds to pay for his flight and for him to stay in London for a week. Besides, I felt this first time around it was better that I took the trip alone. Returning alone the following year was bittersweet. I was looking forward to seeing the city and colleagues again; I regretted that Steve wouldn't have the chance to ever share any of it with me.

The night before returning to the States was Saturday night, but I didn't really feel up to heading into the city. Still I felt like being around gay people. Not particularly interested in meeting anyone, I downed my soda and prepared to head back to the hotel. I was starting to zip up my bomber jacket when off to the side someone asked me for a "fag." I turned to see a young kid I'd noticed earlier. No sooner had I opened my mouth to say "No," than I was almost derisively identified as a "Yank." I thought this is some way to begin a conversation. Two people with seemingly nothing in common and yet we ended up becoming good friends. Between the time we left the pub and hours later when we fell asleep in my hotel room, we exposed each other to some of the painful experiences we had gone through. He put his arms around me while I told him about my late lover; I held him close as he related a childhood of hardship and poverty, with no prospects for much improvement in the future. The sex was not particularly memorable, but the telling and the tears were cathartic.

Mark and I corresponded several times over the following year. He got detailed, word-processed descriptions of my life in New York; I got less elaborate information from him on postcards or brief hand-written letters. Short or long, those letters conveyed the strongest emotional feelings either of us had at the time. I was two decades older than Mark; we came from different cultures; our lifestyles were widely divergent; three thousand miles of ocean separated us; and yet our words were comforting, bonding. A little bit more than a year after Steve's death I had a feeling of warmth and caring for someone again. Mark responded similarly. Uncharacteristically, Mark took into consideration all the factors working against a long-term romantic relationship developing between us, not to mention the possibility that either one of us might meet someone else during our long periods of separation.

Eventually, we decided to see what would happen; to see if we would continue to grow closer together. While I turned my employment search eastward, to London, back in New York I was undergoing changes in my social relationships. Over the preceding year my friends and close acquaintances had adjusted to my being a single man and no longer one part of a couple. I got varying reactions to my decision to relocate; no one was very pleased about my decision. Some friends wondered if I wanted to move to London because Mark was there. Almost everyone thought it strange that I should consider having a relationship with someone so young and so different from me. Not that they gave much hope to a transatlantic affair withstanding the obvious obstacles.

Their concern was appreciated; however their precautions weren't necessary. I think deep down both Mark and I knew that there wasn't much mileage in an affair between us. Mark had expressed his doubts right off the bat. I told myself I was open to the possibility we might work it out, but always in the back of my mind was the dread that try as I might to control my urge to force conventionality on him, I would end up prodding, coaching, and daddying Mark into being the adult I thought he should be. It might work for some guys, but it was not the kind of relationship I wanted. It was difficult, but during one subsequent trip to Britain I put an end to any fantasy Mark or I had that we would be more than good friends.

Workouts have been part of my routine since I was an overweight teenager in The Bronx. I graduated from weights in my bedroom to a universal in the college field house. Workouts were never easy, but they were always fun because of the group of guys I came to know at either of the gyms I was a member of since college. I only saw most of the guys at the gym, but for several of us the companionship extended outside. The wonder is not that I should find love at the gym, but that for all the time that I spend there that it had not happened earlier. As has always happened in the past with me, without the thought of pursuing romance in my mind, I met a man. I met one lover by striking up a conversation in a gay bar, while shared political convictions and activism was the basis for my other relationship. Neither time had I been looking to find a lover. Still, in both cases, I was someplace where there were gay men. Not only had I never had a relationship with someone from the gym, but I hadn't even dated anyone from the gym for most of the two-plus decades I'd been working out in New York. It didn't even seem like an avenue for romance until several months after Steve's death.

Until two years ago, I'd never thought of going out with someone from the gym. Of course, I'd been in two long-term relationships for most of the time I'd been going to the gym in New York. It took me a while of being alone, trying to figure out how to meet someone, before I realized that I could ask out some of the guys at the gym I found attractive and that they might possibly be interested in dating. So I asked. Well, not that forward, and not that often. But enough, so that I went out on a couple of dates. Dinners, brunch, a movie. It was like being a teen-ager again, although as a teen my romantic life had been a dud. Indeed now, unlike my experiences as a teen-ager, I was successful sharing the company of someone else. Not anxious about whether I was going to score. If we had a good meal and some enjoyable conversation that was all I needed. I saw some of the guys I dated once or twice; without enough in common to maintain a more serious relationship we accepted the realities that would keep us as gym buddies. A couple, I dated periodically over the course of several months. One I was seeing fairly regularly. It was during the time that I was seeing the one guy steady that I experienced a sensation I'd never felt before.

Many romantic plots have revolved around a protagonist swearing off romance until all of a sudden they hear "bells and whistles" and see "fireworks." I'd always thought it was an amusing plot device, but a bit of stretch. Perhaps love grew to a fullness; it didn't begin with a crescendo. That's what I thought until one evening at the gym when I noticed an attractive guy working out with one of the trainers. I'd never seen this one before. He was handsome, but there was something else about him, something beyond good looks. Though he was probably close to my age (a definite plus), he exuded an innocent, sincere quality. And not a word had been exchanged between us. Just watching his body movements and his smile struck me. Like a chime. Like a bell. I'm sure I knew I was in love, because all I could see were pyrotechnics when I looked at Doug. He aroused feelings of bliss instantly. Passion, yes, but more than a sexual attraction. Even before we first spoke, I just enjoyed being in the same space with him. I couldn't believe I was feeling these emotions. Two years before, I had felt that there was such an immense gap in the center of my being that it could never be filled again. Slowly over time I'd been able to balance myself. I'd established myself as a single gay man in the eyes of old and new friends, and most importantly in my own eyes. I had learned that I could live on my own. After twenty-three years, I could see who I was without compromise. I was dating, yet I wasn't set on settling down with anyone. Not yet. If ever. I was enjoying being on my own. I'd gone beyond accepting that I might have to live the rest of my life alone; I honestly enjoyed my new status.

Suddenly, I was confronted with a predicament. Actually, a couple of predicaments. The single life had opened new possibilities to me. I had greater employment options. Risk-taking was not compromised by anyone else's welfare. Forced to make my own decisions about everything I did, I had gotten in closer touch with my likes and dislikes. I was filling in a lot of colorless areas about me in my own mind. Nonetheless, I couldn't deny (to myself) that I was more than interested in Doug. Quite frankly, employment options, risk-taking, moving to San Francisco or London, it all went out of my head when I saw Doug.

There was one complication. I was seeing another man. A very nice man who I'd shared some lovely times with over the summer, into the early fall. Our relationship was cruising along, no major bumps. That is until now. Doug and I exchanged a few words since the first time I'd noticed him. I didn't know if he felt the same way I did about him, but I sensed he saw us moving beyond being gym buddies too. I would have felt guilty asking him out, so I tried to convince myself that I was mistaken about his feelings. Still, when he approached me one evening while I finished a set I was certain of his intentions. If Doug had asked me would I like to go on a date, I think I would have answered yes right away. Instead he asked if I was seeing anyone. Before I could think of saying something less definitive I told him yes, I was seeing someone. He may have been disappointed; I was crushed. "What am I saying. No, no! Wait a minute, I didn't mean it. I do want to go out on a date with you.

Clayborne, you idiot." If he'd only ask me again. Doug went back to working out. I could have kicked myself.

Days later, I continued to hope that Doug would give me another chance. We were still acknowledging each other at the gym with smiles and small talk. I didn't know how Doug would have felt about going out on a date with a guy who was seeing someone else, but I didn't want to risk putting him off me, even as a friend. I hoped that he could see how much I liked him, and maybe we could get together as friends. Sometimes when you wish hard enough for something, it happens. Several weeks after first asking me for a date, Doug decided to give it a try again. He told me that he knew I was seeing someone, but did that mean that I wouldn't go out for a meal—say after the gym. (Thank you, God) No hesitation this time, I knew I'd never have this opportunity again. We decided to meet the following Sunday for brunch. When we did get together for that first date, conversation came easily and the time went by quickly. By the time we finished and got ready to part we'd agreed that it would be nice to do it again.

My life has taken such a different course than I would have dreamed of four years ago when I saw myself running alone in that void. I very rarely think about the turmoil I went through back then. I don't avoid it; it just doesn't come to mind very often. I've wondered, does this make me insensitive, a superficial person? "No!" I was devastated by the death of a lover. I couldn't imagine how something like it had happened to me, but I never thought that I wouldn't go on. As in that dream I had no intentions of stopping, of standing still. I didn't know where I'd be going, but I did know that I would move forward. It has taken several years for me to reorganize myself; many of my plans did not materialize. I'm working at the same job. Happily, after a particularly rough period a change in administration offers me a lot of the professional development I've desired for so long. As much as I know I could live on the West Coast or in the UK, I've given up all thoughts of moving to San Francisco or London. I try to keep up with old friends. Separated by the Hudson, I check in with Tony almost everyday by telephone to keep in close contact with him and his new lover, Roy. As for Debra, I don't speak to her as often given her peripatetic schedule; but between her criss-crossing the country and the globe we're in-touch by email and cellular phone. Now and then I'm in touch with other old friends. Most satisfying, Doug and I are sharing our lives together. After a courtship which soon found us spending just about every night of the week together, we decided that we didn't want to live apart. I moved into his apartment this year formally making it our home. In the process, I sold or gave away most of my furnishings and household appliances, separating me further from my past.

As much as anything I was ready to make an unqualified commitment to this relationship. Doug is everything I thought he was the first time I saw him. I kid him about being far more experienced than his innocent looks project, yet for all his intelligence, worldliness, and professional expertise I'm awed by his lack of guile and contempt. Not to say that he is naive. Caring and tactful, he can still be contemplative and candid. Nor have I shared so much with anyone, from politics to knowing the theme songs of sixties TV themes–not many people I know remember "Grindl," let alone the theme music. Besides, his cat has not only grown to tolerate me, but accepts me as Daddy Jon. I never gave thought to my ideal man, and Doug would tell me that he's not ideal; yet, he comes as close as anything I would have imagined or dreamed.

Four years ago, I never dreamed that my life would have moved on to this wonderful stage. Not long after Steve died, the recurring dream stopped suddenly. The last time I recall the dream I was running all alone through the dark–nothing behind me and nothing ahead of me. I remember I tried to envision the dream appearing at least once more. I pictured myself jogging down a country lane effortlessly, in the sunshine; fields of beautiful flowers on one side and a gentle brook on the other. But that dream never came. Instead something much better happened. I got on with my life.

Trading Places:
A Hillside Chat with Don Bachardy

Eric Gutierrez

The house isn't visible from the road. It clings to the canyon in Santa Monica on the side where the sun can be seen setting beyond the breakers of the Pacific. Wind chimes and the occasional automotive static from the road below float through the airy but modest rooms. Don Bachardy, 62, silver-haired and beaming, verbally catalogs the art covering every available wall surface.

A familiar image reproduced as a postcard of writer Christopher Isherwood, Bachardy's lover for 33 years, hangs in the kitchen. The length of "Hockney Hall," from the dining room, past both bedrooms, the bathroom and into Isherwood's old study, is covered floor to ceiling with gouaches and sketches by friend and artist David Hockney. A particularly striking early '80s photo collage outside the bathroom door depicts the couple in the living room of what Bachardy calls "this sacred house." The scene is virtually identical to where we sit today, fifteen years later. Except that Isherwood died in January 1986 of prostate cancer at the age of 81. And Bachardy, chattering amiably, pouring iced tea, now occupies the chair where his celebrated lover had sat mutely charming the camera.

Eric Gutierrez is a Los Angeles-based screen and fiction writer. He currently sits on the editorial board of *OUT* magazine and on the Board of Directors of OUTFEST: The Los Angeles Gay & Lesbian Film Festival.

[Haworth co-indexing entry note]: "Trading Places: A Hillside Chat with Don Bachardy." Gutierrez, Eric. Co-published simultaneously in *Journal of Gay & Lesbian Social Services* (The Haworth Press, Inc.) Vol. 7, No. 2, 1997, pp. 101-111; and: *Gay Widowers: Life After the Death of a Partner* (ed: Michael Shernoff) The Haworth Press, Inc., 1997, pp. 101-111; and: *Gay Widowers: Life After the Death of a Partner* (ed: Michael Shernoff) The Harrington Park Press, an imprint of The Haworth Press, Inc., 1997, pp. 101-111. Single or multiple copies of this article are available for a fee from The Haworth Document Delivery Service [1-800-342-9678, 9:00 a.m. - 5:00 p.m. (EST). E-mail address: getinfo@ haworth.com].

The seating arrangement is telling. Bachardy, who at 18 was thirty years younger than Isherwood when they met, recently celebrated his ninth anniversary with Tim Hilton, twenty-six years his junior. No sketches or photos of him are readily visible.

Gusts of wind sweep through the house and there's a crash in another room. As he races to see what's happened there's still a graceful boyishness about him. A huge wooden mask has blown off the wall, disturbing the calm of this residential shrine.

Although Bachardy has been invited, indeed, implored to talk about himself and the course of his life after Isherwood's death, he constantly refers to "Chris," partly out of gratitude and deference to his legacy but also because one feels that it's an ingrained perspective after a lifetime defined and guided by the writer.

ERIC GUTIERREZ: Thinking back, when did you first understand how your life would be different after Chris' death?

DON BACHARDY: I didn't know what it would be like. I'm not good at guessing how I'll feel or behave in the future. I'd rather wait to see what I'll do. So I never had any plans for after Chris was gone.

It was easier for me than it is for a lot of men because there was a very great age difference between Chris and me so it wasn't as though the idea had never occurred to me that he would die first. I had a lot of time to get used to the idea of being without him.

He got very sick in the last months, and it was harrowing for us both. By the time he died I was glad for both of us. I knew it was a great relief for him and for me too. It was after that the deep grieving, the deep sense of loss, came to me.

EG: Was there anything in particular right after he died that helped lay the foundation for your new life without him?

DB: What I did in those first months after his death was begin to read his diaries. These diaries of his were a great help. He realized they would help me. He himself had foreseen my reading them. Whole passages are addressed to me: "Don, I know that you will be reading this after I am dead."

Although I never thought about it, made a plan, or said "that's what I'm going to do," the very night of the day he died, like a dog on scent, I went right to his desk. I always knew where he kept his diaries although I never read them, I took the first volume to bed with me and that first night began reading.

He left twelve thick volumes and I read them very slowly. I read them in reverse chronological order. Starting with the last, I worked back in time to his descriptions of our first meetings, and beyond that into the 1940s and finally to his arrival in this country in 1939, when his diaries begin. It took me months and was the perfect therapy for me. That, and my own diary. In fact the first bit of advice he gave me in the first weeks we knew each other was to keep a diary. He never gave me bad advice and even then when I was 18 I realized he was telling me something important and I began a diary that first year. So, I had two written accounts of our thirty-three years together to inform me.

EG: Was there anything else besides his diaries and your own that helped you make peace with the process of Chris's death, grieving, and moving on?

DB: Yes, I threw myself back into work. That year alone I produced five portfolios that were thick of sheets of drawings. That first year without him was my busiest year as an artist. My work has always been source of support for me. It was wonderful to have that outlet. During the last six months of Chris's life he was my only subject. I worked with him almost daily and often did as many as ten or twelve drawings in a day—clothed, nude, sitting up in bed, sleeping, whatever he was doing. It was the intensest way of being with him—looking at him, inspecting him closely. My work always involves a form of identification with my subject.

Drawing Chris as he was dying made it seem like his dying was something that we were doing together. Challenging myself as I did with all the drawings of him really helped me to get on with it. It helps enormously to be very very busy.

EG: What was it like living alone for the first time in thirty-three years?

DB: My instinct was to keep myself too busy to acknowledge my aloneness. I scheduled all day sittings five, six sometimes seven days a week. Driving myself like that helped me enormously.

Well, there was no point in wailing and hitting my head against the wall. Whose fault was it? Those are the rules of the game. To whom was I to complain? So I just better go out and help myself.

EG: Were you ever lonely?

DB: My work has always been a great foundation for me. There was no excuse for not doing it. I only work from life, I'm never alone when I'm working. So my sittings provided me with company everyday, whenever I'm working I'm with somebody. When he was gone it seemed to me perfectly natural to set up sittings everyday because then I would have company everyday. Yes, it was lonely in the house at night. (chokes up) I remember coming home, at night, was sometimes difficult . . . (long silence) because we used to make little cries, little noises to each other. (smiles, voice cracks) I'd make a call as I came in the front door and if he were home he'd give me back the call. (laughs, smiles) Yes, I miss that.

EG: It sounds as if you still miss your life together.

DB: (quickly dismissive) Well, you know, I haven't thought of that in a while and you asked me what I missed and that's something that occurred to me. Yes, it was very good. But my loneliness wasn't constant. Sometimes it came only at the end of a day when I'd spent hours and hours working quite happily in the studio with somebody. And the keen concentration required for my work is so demanding that it doesn't leave time to say, "oh, I'm lonely or I've lost somebody dear to me." I just had to get on with the job. My instinct was right just to pile on the work for myself and get on with it.

EG: What lessons have you learned since Chris died that have sustained you in terms of going on with your own life?

DB: In terms of going on with my life? (thoughtful pause) I learned so much from Chris. It would have been very selfish if I didn't share that with someone else. I knew Chris would want me to find somebody. We talked a lot of what I would do once he was gone. We used to joke that he'd live just long enough that I'd be a hideous old wreck when he died and nobody would want me. When we were done laughing, he'd assure me that yes, I would find somebody else.

EG: How much did you date after Chris' death and before Tim?

DB: Chris told me that when he was single before I met him, he kept a little stable of friends who were available as bed partners. So, I took another page from Chris's book. He had a few numbers he could call and I used that as an example for myself. Probably as soon as the second or third month after Chris' death, I found myself fairly often spending the night with one of three young men. I asked myself what would please Chris most; me sitting around mooning and feeling lonely or going out and having a good time and sharing what he taught me with others? Of course there was no question. I didn't owe him any kind of widows weeds. That would have disappointed him.

EG: For the year and a half between your relationships with Chris and Tim, what was it like to be single for the first time in your adult life?

DB: It was rather exciting. In 1986 I was 51 and I looked pretty good for my early fifties. I keep coming back to Chris as an example. He taught me that fun in life didn't have to end because one's middle aged. It was an adventure being on my own.

EG: What was different?

DB: At first the house seemed lonely and darker than it had been before. Then I realized I didn't have to come home alone. There were friends I could invite to spend the night with me and sometimes they did and we slept in the same bed that I'd slept in with Chris. That didn't seem to me unnatural or any kind of sacrilege. I knew it would have pleased him.

Two to three months after Chris died, I got very serious about a sweet young man from the USC film department who was about 22. Our romance went on a good year until something startling happened that was absolutely outside of my experience. He got born again and suddenly changed his attitude towards me. Overnight I became for him a horrible villain, a dirty old man who only wanted his body, was leading him into a life of sin. He eventually got over that idea, but it ended our lovemaking.

EG: Did the friends and intimates you shared with Chris support this chapter of your life or did they somehow resent it?

DB: Of course a lot of my friends knew me in my life with Chris and there were adjustments to be made. Any new love is always compared to the previous one. Whether or not you notice such comparisons being made, you know that they must exist.

EG: How did you handle that?

DB: Again, I take my lead from Chris. It's never been easy for a man of forty-eight to take on an eighteen year old. And in 1953? Boy. A lot of Chris's friends thought he'd lost his mind, it was a middle aged folly. His best woman friend thought he was making such an ass of himself and made her disapproval clear to us both. Do you know, he eventually broke with her and never saw her again? He said, "if she were really my friend she would cheer me on and be glad if I found somebody I care about." So he realized that she really didn't have his best interests at heart and was only concerned about appearances. She winced at Chris's exposing such distinguished friends of his as the Stravinskys and the Huxleys to a nonentity such as I was in her eyes.

EG: And your friends had your best interests at heart?

DB: Most of my good friends took to Tim immediately, and he made it easy for them because he's a great guy–intelligent, charming, witty, much more gregarious than I, and gorgeous, too. There was amazingly little talk behind my back. Everybody seemed really pleased that I'd found somebody to love. They sincerely liked him right away. He's so much himself, so charming, it was easy for them to adjust to him. In many ways, he's so unlike Chris. Lucky for me I had the sense not to try to fill Chris's shoes but found someone different in almost every way.

EG: Were there times then when perhaps you made comparisons?

DB: I wasn't tempted to because I really compared Tim to myself as a young man more than to Chris. That's what's fascinating for me. As well as an unpredictable adventure in itself, my relationship with Tim illuminates for me my life with Chris. So many times I've found myself in situations with Tim which were very similar to ones I'd experienced with Chris, but now I was Chris's age and seeing them from his point of view. So often I've said to myself as if I were talking with Chris, "Oh, *that's* what our misunderstanding was about, *that's* why there was a conflict, *that's* how you felt!"

Since the age difference between Tim and me is almost as great–twenty-six instead of thirty years–as the difference between Chris and me many echoes of my life with Chris sounded in my head. Continually I got insights into things that had happened between Chris and me that I never really fully understood until I was reexperiencing them with Tim. During those early years with Tim I kept a very detailed record of our life together. I'd never before written so much in my diary. Here were all these similar situations occurring or reoccurring. It was endlessly fascinating. My diary entries were as much about Chris as about Tim and me. It was a wonderful way and sometimes almost spooky reliving my past, but this time playing Chris's part.

EG: Was that an easy transition to make?

DB: There were all kinds of adjustments for me to make, too. For example Chris had an appreciation of music but it wasn't often played in this house. To him, words were music. And I went along. He couldn't work if music was being played or if the radio was on. So when I felt like listening to music I went out to my studio. But then Tim moves in to the house with his vast record collection and suddenly there was music or the radio playing all the time, a totally new experience for me. But if you love somebody you love what it is that makes them happy. I know that Tim's music makes him happy. So I adjusted to it and found I could even write when he plays music. Before that I would have sworn I couldn't do that.

EG: Tell me about this new relationship.

DB: Tim is an architect from Oregon, and he's big—six foot two, not small and compact like Chris. Soon after we met he started to come and sit for me. That's a wonderful way of getting to know somebody. This is our ninth year in August, all being well. We met in early June of '86 and Chris died on the fourth of January in 1986. We met at the thirtieth birthday party of a mutual friend and knew each other nearly a year and a half before there was any real intimacy between us. It didn't occur to me that such a thing might be possible from his point of view and when he made it clear that it was . . . we progressed rapidly.

EG: You've been in the unique situation of being with someone older than you, whose death you say you've been unconsciously preparing for from the time you were 18, and now on the other side with someone younger than you. How does it affect your perspective being one part of a couple where you anticipate your lover dying before you and now trading places so that, chronology being what it is, the order might be reversed?

DB: Chris was unique. I knew I could never find anybody who could play his role to my satisfaction so I took on that role myself. Chris was the best role model for anyone worried about aging because he managed to grow old without scaring the shit out of everybody. I found a younger man to play a part similar to the one I played with Chris. He gave me a lot of confidence. It was all such good help once he was gone. To see someone getting old and doing it well is the best experience a young person can have. It was one of the great advantages Chris afforded me. Now I'm trying to do the same for Tim.

EG: Since so much of your life was defined by Chris, how have you come to define yourself after his death?

DB: I was already an artist in my own right long before Chris died, and I've continued to be that, all the more so now. I found capacities in myself for many new experiences, such as being the older party in an intimate relationship. I found whole sides of myself that were new to me. It was new to me to be the older party in an intimate relationship. For years and years with Chris I was invariably the youngest person in any group we were in. Now with Tim I'm most often the oldest person, and I know how to play that part from observing Chris. I even enjoy it and already feel slightly resentful if somebody older comes into the room, as though I were being upstaged.

EG: How about discoveries about yourself, as an individual, not in terms of Tim or Chris?

DB: You mean, besides discovering my adaptability to living with Tim? To me that was, and still is, a big discovery about myself as an individual. I have learned that I can relinquish the spotlight, give someone else the lead. I was really very bossy with Chris. But I've learned, as Chris did with me, to regard deferring to Tim as a luxury. I didn't think I had it in me. Come to think of it, I do adapt to my sitters. I soak up their moods, adjust to their rhythm of movement, identify with their physical looks and personalities. I was surprised by my powers of adaptability. I amazed myself how I was able to adapt to Tim in so many ways. But if you love somebody adaptation comes easily. You want to please the one you love so the changes you're making have a very real goal, the pleasure of the person you love. If he's pleased then I'm pleased.

EG: OK, think about it in terms of when you were single for the first time, not having to take someone else into consideration. What did you discover about yourself being by yourself?

DB: Tim and I did kind of go headlong into this thing. After I realized that I'd lost my young USC film student to Jesus Christ, I immediately found Tim. Almost immediately we started spending every night together. In less than three months Tim was moving into this house. Right before I had a failure of nerve but then of course, what do I remember? Chris at 48 doing exactly the same thing with me, an 18 year old. So, I thought, if Chris could do it, maybe why couldn't I? At least Tim was twenty-six, and I was still only fifty-two—a mere chicken it seems now!

EG: Was that failure of nerve really about not knowing Tim that well or just not being ready yet?

DB: I didn't know. Some of both I guess. I suddenly felt that I was going into unknown territory. Then I saw that it was really territory that I knew quite well, only seen from a different perspective—through Chris's spectacles as it were. Often in difficult situations with Tim, I ask myself, what would Chris do? And I always get an answer. If I concentrate and put him in the position I'm in, I always get a message from him.

EG: Do you ever disagree with the message?

DB: No, because, you see, I know how sound Chris was.

EG: There have never been times when you thought although Chris may have done it one way, you prefer to do it another?

DB: It wasn't that I was slavishly following Chris's lead and mindlessly obeying him. We were naturally in sync. We instinctively knew what was best for each other. He asked for my advice, too, you know, and took it often. I wasn't shy about handing it out. In fact, I can be quite sensible. I'm not always blindly pursuing young hunks!

But there were occasions, too, when I didn't follow Chris's advice. Every once in a while, even when you know you're getting good advice, you have to do the reverse just for the hell of it, to prove you can make an independent decision even if it's a wrong one. It just so happened that, when I did ignore his advice, I usually regretted it.

EG: Since so much of your present life is guided by his example, is there something you remember from before your relationship with Chris that has stayed with you, a part of yourself that you think of as defining who you are?

DB: Funny, as a kid I was always a loner. I never had close relationships outside those with my mother and brother and the fantasy ones I indulged in with actors I loved in the movies. In school I never had a confidante or even a particular buddy. It almost seems now as if I were being nurtured in a hothouse until I was ripe to meet Chris. Then I did meet him and suddenly realized that I was a big ferocious fruit, and I've been one ever since.

Going It Alone

John F. Longres

The sun has broken through the January clouds if only for a minute. The red edged nandina glistens and the limbs of the fig tree, heavy with October's nearly ripened fruit, reach up across a barely blue sky. I sit in my chair in the breakfast nook looking across the table at his chair. It has been some fourteen months now and still the morning paper does not quite distract me, though the peek of sun lifts my spirit. Tonight I will go see "The English Patient" and in the same breath a memory: He left the book on the desk one summer evening and told me I would enjoy it, and of course I did. My breath continues to be intertwined with his.

On another gray and much colder January, some twenty-nine years earlier, things were very different. I, already world wise, let out a sigh as I rushed passed him, under the marquee of the State Street theater, on my way to an eight o'clock. What a surprise then that he, an emotional innocent, would be sitting across the reading room table that very afternoon, longing for this moment to occur. He was an American from the heartland just recently back from two years in Spain and I was a Puerto Rican New Yorker who had arrived in Ann Arbor via Los Angeles. He was reading linguistics and I was reading social psychology and both of us were preparing

---

John F. Longres, PhD, is Professor of Social Work at the University of Washington, and has had a long career in social work education and research, and looks forward to the new phase in his life.

[Haworth co-indexing entry note]: "Going It Alone." Longres, John F. Co-published simultaneously in *Journal of Gay & Lesbian Social Services* (The Haworth Press, Inc.) Vol. 7, No. 2, 1997, pp. 113-123; and: *Gay Widowers: Life After the Death of a Partner* (ed: Michael Shernoff) The Haworth Press, Inc., 1997, pp. 113-123; and: *Gay Widowers: Life After the Death of a Partner* (ed: Michael Shernoff) The Harrington Park Press, an imprint of The Haworth Press, Inc., 1997, pp. 113-123. Single or multiple copies of this article are available for a fee from The Haworth Document Delivery Service [1-800-342-9678, 9:00 a.m. - 5:00 p.m. (EST). E-mail address: getinfo@haworth.com].

for pre-lims. He nervously invited me to share a San Miguel he had in his refrigerator and we went off to live happily ever after.

Our studies, and the university careers that followed, bound us together and yet we intended them to be incidental to our lives, more a means than an end. We courted each other with talk of a life of constant travel. He had already been to the Caribbean and to many European countries. I had crisscrossed the United States several times by bus and car and lived a couple of summer stock seasons in Ontario, Canada. I knew a movie star once who told me to live by the rule, "wild abandon, tight control." University careers, we agreed, would provide us with the control we needed to assure our abandon into love and the furthest corners of the globe.

And that's how the friendship started although somewhere along the way it took a different turn more so for me I think. Perhaps I should have seen it coming. I returned to school out of fear of becoming a failure. Even as I approach my 60th, the anxiety provoked by my 21st birthday stands out like no other. I had dropped out of college after my sophomore year and spent two years living in Greenwich Village. At 21, I became frightened I wouldn't make it as an actor and hurried back to school, the only thing that up till then I was really good at. I had no clear idea of my professional alternatives but good grades led to scholarships, that led to doctoral studies that led to Jim. What did I know of a life of a professor? You taught your classes and had your summers, Christmases, and spring breaks off, right?

Ambition soon crept up on us and control eventually came to dominate abandon. In part, it was because we were pretty good at our occupations even as we feigned indifference. We were both sincere about our disciplines and more than willing to do a good job and contribute to our departments. We published and didn't perish, were easily tenured, and eventually received recognition in professional circles.

In the end, however, it was the response of others to our professional success that sucked us deeper into our careers. After I got back from a Fulbright, my Dean made the mistake of telling me I was a "star," a "role model" for the junior professors. Even though the pond was indeed small, I was flattered enough to start expending summers doing research, writing books and articles, and editing a journal. And Jim, of course, was also being shaped by his rewards matching my ascendance rung for rung. Truncated summers became the norm as our trips got shorter and more tied to work. It was in Oslo, after still another paper in Amsterdam, that Jim, four years into his diagnosis, stepped out of the shower and showed me the little purple splotch on the inside of his thigh. I couldn't think of anything to do but kiss it. Although we talked about it wishfully, we never took another trip.

I think I got more caught up in my career than Jim, or perhaps it was because he was dying and knew enough to make the best of what was left. In any event, Jim gave up his career more easily than I would have expected. He collapsed from anemia while giving a lecture on the structure of the English language and was rushed to the hospital. He recovered quickly but, being a very private person, was mortified enough never to return to university life. Undoubtedly it was difficult, but at the end of that spring quarter he shut his office door behind him, taking only two boxes of books and six floppy disks. He went on his third and last sabbatical knowing that he would not return to work even if he managed to survive the year. He simply turned to his inner resources, and as it turned out there were many: reading novels and biographies, raising silk moths, caring for his butterfly garden, listening to classical music, and occasionally tooting his flute or fingering the piano. These gave him solace and strength to the very end.

Even in the years we lived with the knowledge that our life together was ending, I found it easy to drown myself in work. Work became a kind of haven that distracted me from the heartless reality of home. My duty at home was to give him the emotional support he needed to face his fate. It was a labor of love made possible only because Jim was the perfect patient. Moments of panic aside, he was movie-hero strong and worried as much about me as I about him. But it was labor nevertheless. Caring for the dying requires a level of selflessness that is achievable only by fiercely subduing every instinct to flee. I am too self-centered for sainthood, too caught up in my personal needs and as a result I labored in the fear that I would bolt. Work served to anchor me to his side.

Strange as it may seem, those last years were relentlessly tender, if not altogether happy. I think back on memories of inexpressible closeness. I remember most the evening routine; reading till nine; viewing a pre-recorded Nova or Mystery! or a rented tape of a movie we had missed; me massaging first his throbbing temples and then his swollen, purple brown, football sized feet; he purring like a kitten, curled up in the energy of my hands; lifting him into his bed half asleep. In giving as totally as we could, death helped us uncover whatever meaning there may be in life.

In spite of being on the watch for six years, death sneaked in and claimed Jim quickly. He was never bedridden. Although he was wasting away, he was active to the end. He stopped his daily jogging two years before and his daily walks only six months before. He could still manage a walk through the garden plucking a weed or two before exhaustion forced him back to his brown striped chair in the living room, from there to look out on the apple, pear and cherry trees that wrapped us in the changing seasons of our Eden. On Tuesday, the doctor told him the chemotherapy had failed and there was nothing to be done. We were worried, of course, but he seemed fine. On Wednesday at noon he fell ill. He died about seven. It was October and the leaves began to fall.

After his death, career continued to be my haven. I stayed home for about two weeks and found the house too redolent with his being to remain. The longer the hours at work the better. By this time I was administrating more than teaching and pushing paper seemed just the tonic I needed. I became swallowed up in a major report, found new energy for my writing, and managed to convince myself of the importance of the tasks I was doing. I knew well that I would have to balance my life, find a way to bring the abandon back, but after years of tightening control this was not to come easily.

An English friend came to visit Jim and me after the death of his partner. It was July and the flag pole looming high above the dogwood was decked out with an unintentionally wrong-side-up Union Jack and a huge white flag, trumpeting happy birthday in colorful red for all three of us. Our friend said it was the first time he was able to grieve in public, only with us could he openly acknowledge his lover's death. This was not the case for me. As Jim's death approached, both of us received a huge outpouring of support which continued during the months immediately after his death. His mother and brothers and their families and relatives could not have been more considerate. My three sisters and I drew closer, as never before, and all of them crossed the Rockies for Jim's funeral in Missouri. My high school chum, traveling from New York, dropped everything to come to the funeral. The president of the university called to wish me well. Jim's colleagues gathered round and filled the mail with cards and letters. My colleagues did the same, even the straight men in my department wrote thoughtful notes. Our friends, straight and gay and in between, rallied round and proved their worth. The minister who would perform the service called long distance to welcome me to his small town Methodist church and, upon my departure, gave me a book of his poems. My loss was not suffered in a closet.

I think grief is an overused word to explain everything and anything having to do with loss however trivial. But whatever my emotion is, I guess I had (have) a lot. I have always cried at the drop of a sentimental hat yet it may be worse now. Anything remotely having to do with love, happy endings, death, you name it, sets me off. I believe I am also less patient, more easily agitated, and more absentminded. I left a hundred dollar bill and two bags of Starbuck coffee beans on a bus. I had three, thankfully minor, automobile accidents within a year of Jim's death. I climbed the walls on weekends and lost it all on Christmas eve amid a half-heartedly decorated hearth. Yet, I functioned fairly well at work and my blood pressure, after approaching the worrisome zone during his illness, declined to a normal level. I upped the number of miles I was jogging. I played racquetball every Wednesday evening. I dined with friends, joined clubs, volunteered with a grassroots agency.

About two months after Jim's death, I also joined a grief group. The immediate impetus came from an unlikely source. Our neighbors across the lilac hedge were a retired Lutheran minister and his wife. They were a perfectly nice couple but we assumed that, being tied to a fairly conservative church, they would have no part of us. Their cocker spaniel bit Jim when we first moved in and when it died two years later we feared they would have an autopsy. The wife was so distraught over the dog's death that she took our cat and never let him out of her house; we learned she even changed his name. In any event, the minister died of a cancer about a year before

Jim and we went over to pay our respects. So when Jim died, she and I–as two widowed people–had a potential affinity. Sure enough she knocked on the door one day, sincerely wished me good cheer, and told me how helpful a grief group had been to her. She made a special effort to say that there had been "all sorts" of people in the grief group and that I would "fit in."

So off I went to a group but it was such a disaster I left after two sessions. The facilitator, a well-intentioned young man half my age, was caught up in a new age, spirituality trip. His major aim was to get us to do a "talking circle," a technique he had learned from his interest in Native American culture. He was not about to let us simply talk to each other. We each held an eagle feather while we spoke and only when we had finished everything we had to say–everyone else staring silently and attentively–could we pass the feather on and let the next person speak. Grief groups were not for me.

Part of the malaise I felt had to do with my indefinite health status. About ten months after his death, I decided it was time to be re-tested as I had not done so since 1989. While caring for Jim, I had not always taken the necessary gloved precautions largely because it made me feel guilty to think I was afraid of his illness. I also had managed occasional encounters during the years of his sickness, one or two of which were on the gray side of safety.

In the spring of 1987, I came down with the shingles and for the next two years drove us both crazy with an unquenchable fear of having been infected. Jim, to put a stop to my craziness, finally took the initiative and made an appointment for the two of us at the public health clinic. We were interviewed together, each of us admitting indiscretions that we mostly knew about and accepted as a necessary part of our professional absences from each other. We sat side by side as the technician drew our blood, rich red streaming into transparent vials. The next two weeks were impossibly tense but Jim bought us tickets for opening night at the Ice Capades and thereby convinced me I would be celebrating a clean bill of health. When at last the public health worker told me I was negative, I dissolved into a torrent of tears. Still sobbing, he led me to the next room where Jim sat stone faced, like a bust of Caesar against a window full of rain clouds. After several bumbling minutes, the absurd truth got sorted out; my tear ducts drying in an instant.

Jim did his crying later, a deep, quiet, trembling cry. As we lay in bed—my arm under his neck, his head shuddering on my shoulder, turned inwardly toward each other on a just dark June night—I said I was sure they got the test results mixed up, after all we had gone through it together, an easy mistake. He instructed me not to fill him with false hopes as he had to spend his time adjusting and not living a fantasy. Without telling him, I got tested again two weeks later and reconfirmed my negative status on the day of his first clinic visit, when he was informed his T-cell count was 250.

Most of our friends assumed I was positive. Why wouldn't they as even I found the circumstances implausible. But it was nevertheless disconcerting to be confronted with their assumptions, fears, innuendoes, or questions. How does one explain it? Jim and I looked for no explanation. Every once in a while we speculated about why him and not me, but we both saw the dead end in this and simply accepted our happenstance destinies.

It was inevitable, therefore, that I would have myself re-tested. Instead of a sympathetic gay public health worker, the new worker was an apparently heterosexual woman who instructed me on the dangers of not having used gloves and clucked ominously as I described each preoccupation. After a tortured week of waiting, a different worker lectured me on the dangers of unsafe sex even as she announced I was negative. I stopped her mid-sentence, told her this was too emotional a moment for me, got up and walked out the door, my stomach in a knot.

I work on grief through less formal means and I believe I have made the right decision. You have to be careful where you openly acknowledge your loss. One night, at the Friday Night Pot-Luck Club, I overheard the following conversation.

I went on this great kayaking trip last week.

Kayaking? You know Don and I were really into that.

Don?

Yeah, you remember, my partner . . . he died last year.

Oh yeah. . . . yeah, I remember him.

Close friends—those who will know who you are talking about—can be very helpful but even here you have to pick your moments. I think the role of a good friend is to keep you moving forward. There is a thin line between attentiveness and condescension, between sincerity and ritual. I became leery of those who wanted me to express how I "really" felt for when I did open up, it often produced fidgeting on their part or a leap into problem solving advice. All I wanted was a shoulder to cry on. I didn't expect or even want to solve my grief, if that's what it was, and spilling my guts to them often made me feel worse. I found friends helpful when they did what friends ought to do: when they forced me out of myself, made me laugh, invited me to plays and movies, told me about the books they read, debated politics, dined with me, dragged me around to bars and parties, teased me about possible romantic adventures, hooked me up to the virtual realties of cyberspace. I even found it helpful when they complained of their miseries, the better to see that I had no unique claim to mine.

I found special comfort in those who had also experienced the death of a partner. The give and take between us invariably seemed right, seemed settling. This is the potential of a grief group led by someone who understands death and the self-pitying sorrow that follows. An acquaintance who befriended me in the last two years of Jim's life, told me how his father and his lover died in the same week. He warned that AIDS was a marathon, not a sprint, and that I would have to learn to pace myself if I expected to finish the race with some breath left. He sat with me gently in the months after Jim's death and then drifted out of my life like a guardian angel off to help another. A long-time friend from my sophomore year at college re-entered my life unexpectedly. We customarily exchanged Christmas cards and when I wrote him about Jim's death, he immediately wrote back telling me of his friend's recent death. I went down to Los Angeles on two separate occasions and we wallowed in our mutual tragedies, providing blow-by-blow descriptions of the horrors brought on by AIDS and its aftermath, yet simultaneously giving each other the will to go on. No free advice, just the company of two men slowly getting out from under the shadow of death.

Work, or rather career, turned out to be the real challenge and it hit me full brunt just when the northwest skies began to turn their royal summer blue. I accepted an appointment to an administrative position two months before Jim's death. Although by this time a visit to the clinic was a daily routine, he had been living so well with AIDS that we fully believed he had some years left. In accepting the appointment, I did worry about the summers. I remember asking if it were possible to have a ten-month appointment and was told that it might be. Yet, I knew we wouldn't be doing any traveling and so the prospect of spending time in the office in the summer didn't seem an especial burden.

The summer, however, had always been special and not only because we traveled. Summers were also a time of sleeping late and luxuriating in each other's company. Although I can comfortably sleep eight hours, Jim could top ten in a single snore and carry me along with him. A pot of coffee while reading the paper would be followed by a three-mile run and a luscious breakfast, often with our running group. Sooner or later we were in the yard, he in his flower beds and me poking around in the vegetables. Although I could decorate a house, I was a lunkhead in the garden. I could water and pick fruits and vegetables and could even prune a tree or two, mow lawns, and rake leaves but it was Jim who had the designer's eye out-of-doors. He patiently tried to pass on his talents in those last years of summer and encouraged me to read his many gardening books and magazines. I went with him to his garden group and, in preparation, he drilled me with Latin names that, like Mrs. Malaprop, I invariably mangled. He assured me I was ready to maintain the grounds and I fully anticipated giving it a try.

I managed to prune the berry bushes and grapes over a rainier than usual Thanksgiving break. I clipped the roses after President's Day, as he had instructed but, alas, just before an unexpected and very unusual freeze. I reasoned that he hated roses anyway and so it didn't matter what happened to them. In March, I decided to let the fruit trees go without a pruning, I would do them the next year for sure. May came and I managed to roto-till the vegetable patch and fill the large clay pots that flanked the front door with vibrant orange-red geraniums. Things were looking up. In early June, I weeded flower beds but hardly made a dent. I also designed an embankment of sage and grasses but the execution left much to be desired. By mid-June I decided to let the vegetable patch go fallow, it would do the land good I told myself. Then it became clear that I wouldn't be able to revive the red, yellow and blue butterfly garden and the grass kept growing so fast I was spending three hours a week chugging around the two acres of lawn on a tractor.

And all the while the demands at work grew and grew. We had to get the report in by August 14th and through most of June, July and early August I was putting in 12-hour days, six and sometimes seven days a week. A quick cup of coffee in the morning, a cold bowl of cereal, a glance at the paper, and off to work. At night I'd crawl exhausted into his bed, find my spot in his pillow, and comforted by the memory of his lingering scent, fall asleep–only to awaken an hour later and toss and turn the rest of the night listing the things I had to remember to do.

August 15th I was to begin my vacation. I planned a great trip east to visit friends, many from my high school days, in Vermont, Maine and New York. On the 13th, amid the frantic last minute rush to finish the report, my mother suffered a mild heart attack brought on by, among other reasons, my impending eastern vacation. So it was off to a Los Angeles of hospitals, convalescent homes, and a *pobre mamacita* filled with the anxieties of an embittered old age. I returned home to face dried up flower beds and weedy brown grass. As I strolled around, I counted three dead rhododendrons and a defunct mountain laurel. The apple and pears were pocked with worms. The grapes seemed fine, though, and with any luck it appeared I might even have a second crop of purple figs. I promised myself I would get to the berry bushes once the fall rains started.

Going back to work, however, was very difficult. The first week left me drained and for the first time in my life I did not look forward to getting up in the morning. In a moment of decision, I called the benefits office and asked about a possible early retirement. The benefits officer informed me I couldn't retire till I was 62. I could resign, she said, but that would not allow me to be named *emeritus*, and would not allow me to claim the other benefits of a retired professor, the most important of which was the maintenance of my health insurance policy.

I decided to resign anyway but in the next breath I was frozen by the panic of ending my career, losing my status in society, and starting off alone on the path that no one hopes to travel by. I tried to strengthen my resolve. After all, my pension would not be significantly diminished and I could find a health insurance policy on my own. Who needed to be an *emeritus*!

Yet I could not do it even as the days at work grew more onerous. The career, that a year before had seemed the necessary crutch in going it alone, was now the ball and chain that kept me in a past I could not sustain. My life has been terribly fulfilling, even charmed. I have loved and I have been successful in my chosen profession, yet here I was stymied by an unexpected void. Until I am able to see the outlines of a new life, I will have to go through the motions of the old. Yes, the end of my career would have been easier with Jim. With Jim I had a sense of self beyond my occupation. With Jim I had the staff with which to regain the balance of my youth. The reality is, however, that there is no Jim and that I am on this path alone, re-naming myself as I go along.

It would be nice to think that I will love again but if it is to occur, it will be under a different set of hopes and dreams. At the moment, I cling to family for my continuity and focus on friends, new and old, for my companionship. I step down from my administrative duties and arrange for time off. I go about my garden chores, Jim's legacy, but dust off my youthful interests. October is difficult but as its golden leaves turn their murky December brown, I sense some pieces falling into place.

I put the paper down and reach for the phone. A couple of friends agree to join me at the movies. I put on my muddy canvas coat, run my hand across the back of his chair, and head out across the soggy lawn to prune the raspberries. I'm three months late but hell, I'm doing the best I can.

I'm Not Done Yet

Phill Wilson

WEIRD THINGS HAPPEN

It's weird, so very weird. It's probably the weirdest thing you'll ever experience.

The jarring sound of the phone ringing startled me. I wasn't asleep. But, because I hadn't slept in days, I wasn't quite awake either. "Is this the Chris Brownlie Hospice?" asked an unfamiliar voice. "Yeah, I guess so," I stuttered. It was 3:00 in the morning, and all I could wonder was who would be asking such a question at this hour, and in such an insistent tone. "Who is this?" I said. "May I help you?"

"Can you confirm what time Chris Brownlie died," the voice demanded rather than asked. "You've got to be kidding me," I thought. This whole thing had seemed like a dream. I guess this call meant the nightmare had taken an unexpected and unappreciated turn for the worse. "I beg your pardon? Who is this?"

"I'm sorry, this is the *L.A. Times*. I'm on deadline. I already have the obituary. I just need a confirmation of the time."

"Listen, I'm Chris Brownlie's lover. I don't know who you are.

Phill Wilson is Director of the Southern California AIDS Social Policy Archive at the University of Southern California. He also founded the National Black Lesbian and Gay Leadership Forum.

[Haworth co-indexing entry note]: "I'm Not Done Yet." Wilson, Phill. Co-published simultaneously in *Journal of Gay & Lesbian Social Services* (The Haworth Press, Inc.) Vol. 7, No. 2, 1997, pp. 125-136; and: *Gay Widowers: Life After the Death of a Partner* (ed: Michael Shernoff) The Haworth Press, Inc., 1997, pp. 125-136; and: *Gay Widowers: Life After the Death of a Partner* (ed: Michael Shernoff) The Harrington Park Press, an imprint of The Haworth Press, Inc., 1997, pp. 125-136. Single or multiple copies of this article are available for a fee from The Haworth Document Delivery Service [1-800-342-9678, 9:00 a.m. - 5:00 p.m. (EST). E-mail address: getinfo@haworth.com].

But, he's not dead yet, thank you very much. I'll tell you what. When he does die, I'll make sure someone calls you." "Oh, I'm really sorry." This time he stuttered. "I didn't mean . . ."

"I know, I know. I'm sorry, too," I said. "You really need to find a better way to do this." I hung up the phone and quietly went back to my vigil.

I had answered crisply, but inside of me rose a sick sort of panic. Not only was I going to have to go through Chris's death, but even this would not be the end of this for me. People were going to be asking me questions that I would have to answer again and again, and I would be forced to relive this nightmare forever. Even when it was over, it wouldn't be over.

I sat there and watched him. I don't think I cried that night. I just sat there in that chair, next to Chris's bed. I just sat in that chair and I started to remember. I don't remember all the places my mind took me that night. But I gladly went. I knew what was going to happen. And trucking off into our nostalgic past was better than staring unflinchingly into what seemed to be my desolate future.

THE BEGINNING

It's feeling cheated because it was supposed to be forever and it was only ten years!

I met Chris Brownlie in 1980, at Club baths in Chicago. I was twenty-three years old, engaged to be married and had never had sex with a man before. Chris was not what one would call a classic beauty. Although through my heart's eye, he was the most beautiful man in the world. He had these bow legs. I had never seen a white boy with bow legs before. He was unbelievably skinny (although skinny was in, in 1980) with this head of hair that looked like a lion's mane, and he had the most magnificent smile I had ever seen. And those eyes, "those eyes so true." Chris's eyes were full of love and passion and life. He grabbed me with those eyes and he didn't let go until he closed them for the last time, the day he died, ten years later.

THE END

It's the breaking of your heart every time you have to leave him in the hospital. It's having to leave him in the hospital too often. It's being a member of the team that makes the decisions about his care. It's making the final decisions all by yourself.

It's the echo of his voice in your ear on the eve of his death when he says to you "Take me home!" It's the echo of your voice in the hollow of your heart created by the pain of the loss.

It's saying, "I'm fine. I'll take care of everything. I'll handle it." It's discovering you are not fine. You can't take care of anything, and this time you can't handle it.

It's feeling the pain and knowing each bit of hurt is a celebration of the love you feel for each other. It's the chuckle in his voice when he awakes from the coma in middle of the night to tell you he loves you. It's telling him you love him as he takes his last breath.

It's holding him and feeling the warmness of his life leave his body.

It's funny how memory works. I remember lots of things about Chris and our relationship. I remember the places we lived, the vacations we took, conversations we had. But, I live or relive two events over and over again—the day we met and the day he died.

The nurse woke me up around five thirty in the morning. I had been asleep for about three hours. The house seemed strange. I couldn't tell why exactly. Maybe it was because I had spent so little time at home over the previous months. Maybe because I knew that in a few minutes this house, our home would be forever changed. I got up, went to the bathroom to wash my face and walked into the other bedroom. Our best friends were standing around the bed watching as Chris lay sleeping.

I had done the right thing to bring him home. Even though no one had agreed with me. But I didn't have any choice. Chris woke up from his coma one day, he looked at me and said, "Take me home." Everyone tried to convince me that it was the metaphorical "take me home." Maybe it was. But it was also the literal take me home. He wanted to die at home, and he knew that I needed him to die at our house, in the home that we had created together. I needed to say goodbye to him in our space. I needed to have that to hold onto in the weeks, months and years that would follow; and he wanted to give me that gift.

I got in the bed with him. I stroked his forehead. I put my lips to his ear and sang "Let me call you sweetheart I'm in love with you. Keep your love light burning in your eyes so true. Let me call you sweet heart. I'm in love with you."

"O.K. sweet heart," I said, "it's time. I'm ready. I'm going to be O.K."

His body seemed to relax. He took three more breaths. And then he didn't take another. I asked Mary, Chris's best friend, to sing "Summertime" from *Porgy and Bess*. Mary has this beautiful soprano voice and her voice and Chris's spirit filled the room. I moved down to the foot of the bed so I could hold his feet. As they began to cool, I stroked his ankles and then, as they in turn cooled, his knees. I put my hands on his stomach. Finally the only warm place left on his body was his chest. I laid my head there with my eyes closed until I could feel the last bit of warmth leave his body. I opened my eyes to see the sun peeking through the window of the bedroom. The night was over and Chris was gone.

Chris had AIDS for 33 months. Through it all I never saw myself without him. I never prepared for being a widower. I was almost 34 years old the morning Chris died and I couldn't remember how it felt to not be with him. As I would realize in the coming months, I had lived my entire Gay life with Chris. Now, for the first time, I was a single gay man. I had no experience at being single. I didn't know what it meant to be single. I didn't know how to do "single." Quite frankly, I didn't want to be single. But there I was–34, single HIV positive, and alone.

WHAT IS GRIEF?

It's driving down the freeway and being blinded by your tears. It's not knowing that you are crying. It's wondering what will happen to you when your time comes and he's not there to send you home. It's knowing he will be there.

It's the numbness, the panic, the fear, the sadness. It's the blind rage over what's happening to you.

People ask me if Chris and I had a perfect relationship. I don't think any relationship is perfect, or maybe every relationship where two people really love each other is perfect.

I experienced three very distinct kinds of grief: intense pain; profound confusion; feeling lost. There were the things that I was acutely aware of as they happened. There were other times when I felt something or knew intuitively that I was going through something emotionally, but I was not able to determine exactly what. I called this experience "my screaming subconscious" or my "back brain consciousness." Finally there were times when I had no idea what or if anything was going on inside of me. During this time I would focus on getting through the day. When the day was too much to handle, I would go to the hour or minute, or, at times, the second. I would look for and find whatever measure of time I could handle.

It's really important to remember that grief is not sadness. My friend Mark, whose lover died in 1992, described grief as this always unpredictable storm of emotions where he kept being surprised, first of all at just at how long it lasted, and second of all at what kind of new unpleasant emotions were going to sort of jump out of him from some corner of his soul.

Mark also talked about a disturbing sexualized grief that manifested itself in an unfamiliar horniness. Mark told me "I would go searching for sex, and the urge was more insistent and consuming than ever before. At some level, I knew it wasn't about desire, or even wanting sex. It was a weird and disorienting way of missing him, longing for him, grieving for him."

Often I didn't know what to do with my grief. I did know how to work. I could do that. And so I did. Chris died at 6:00 on November 28, 1989. By 10:30 I was in my office. I have no real memories of those days, but I worked every day from the end of November until February.

In the beginning, I thought about as little as possible. There was this automatic pilot thing going on. There were really a lot of things that had to get done–funeral plans, burial plans, cremation, insurance, death notification. Some of these things are a part of the ritual that allowed me time to create a distance, and helped me get through the excruciating pain of the loss. Because I was caught up in this make busy stuff, I didn't have time to realize what was happening. Unfortunately, the "make busy" ended. There came a time when there was no more minutia, and try as I might to avoid them, there were the quiet times. That's when all of sudden I realized that he's dead. He was not coming back. I was all alone. There were people who said I was not really alone. But during those moments I was really, most definitely alone!

The morning that Chris died, after the paramedics took him, as the hearse drove away, I stood there and watched the cars go by–back and forth, back and forth. I remember thinking how weird it was, something had happened to me that was so traumatic that nothing would ever be the same again, and yet, as I watched the cars go by, it seemed as though to the rest of the world everything was the same. I realized that to the rest of the world everything was the same. I walk back into the house, my house now, and it was empty. The cats were there. I was there. Maybe even some of our friends were still there. I don't remember. But the house was still empty.

MISSING HIM

It's remembering in the middle of the day and feeling as if it were happening all over again. It's the loneliness, because you have no other friend like him.

It's calling your landlord to find out how much is the rent or calling the bank to find out what's your balance; because he did those things.

It's sitting at home and wondering what's keeping him because you forgot he's not coming home. It's keeping the tape on the answering machine because it is a way of hearing his voice.

It's being glad to return home after a trip because you know the cats miss him nearly as much as you do. It's keeping his

*drivers license, wearing both of your wedding bands, isolating
yourself from family and friends; because you don't know what
else to do.*

The night after Chris died, I had this dream. In the dream, Chris
and I were coming out of 5P21 (the LA County AIDS ward). As we
entered the parking lot we realized that we didn't remember where
we had left the car. I would see the car in one place. Chris would see
it in another space. I would go over to the right and Chris would go
to the left. When I got to the spot where I thought the car was, it
would not be there. In the course of this dream, we found ourselves
further and further apart. As the dream continued the parking lot got
larger and larger, and fuller and fuller until the lot was absolutely
packed. Finally, Chris was nowhere in sight.

I still want to tell him things, even today, six years later. But in
the beginning I would just talk to him, sometimes in my head,
sometimes out loud. I would talk to him as if he were there, as if he
were in the bed with me or on the sofa. Or I would be at work and I
would want to call him. I would pick up the phone to say, "Hey, did
you read this or that? Turn on CNN," or, "What would you like to
do tonight?" That went on for months.

DATING AGAIN

It's wishing he were here. It's knowing that he is.

I think that following the death of a partner people come to a
determination of how to start dating again by different means. Some
people don't start dating again until some artificially imposed time
passes (six, months, two years, etc.). Chris taught me how to build a
relationship based in the present, to focus on the day. That lesson
was invaluable in helping me to decide when and how to begin to
date again. There was a simple rule. If the experience was comfortable, I repeated it. If it were not, I did not. I also had a fundamental
belief that my relationship with Chris was such that he wanted me
to be happy (that was the big message of our relationship) and I felt
that this was true of my moving on. Chris would want me to be
happy. That certainly has been helpful. I've had two relationships

since Chris died. My first was with Brad. He was not threatened by Chris. Possibly because Chris's death was relatively new, and my grieving process was integrated into the development of our relationship.

I met Brad four months after Chris's death. Shortly after meeting him, I went to Europe. Starting the relationship with Brad was my first big decision after Chris's death. I had not yet developed a new decision making process. So I stayed with what I knew. I went to Chris. One rainy afternoon I found myself outside the chapel at the London Lighthouse. The chapel was empty and I sat down and had a quiet discussion with Chris. I told him about Brad. I told him how I felt. I asked him what he thought. I felt his presence. Chris had been an atheist for most of his adult life. I could hear him chuckle and say, "This is a fine place for you to decide to have a conversation with me." It was as if he was telling me to relax and stop looking for the right answer or waiting for the right time. When I returned to Los Angeles I knew that Brad and I would work it out, and whatever we decided would be fine with Chris.

It took about eight more months before Brad and I actually became a couple. Being in love with Brad was very good for me. In some ways having a good relationship or having someone that I cared about and that I think cared about me was a part of healing. It was nice to have fun romantic times with him. I knew there were things that I experienced in my relationship with Chris that I wanted to continue to experience in my relationship with Brad. I was aware of the differences between Brad and Chris. I didn't want to compare them, but I couldn't help but compare them. Brad had to compete with this mythical person. It would have been one thing to compete with an alive person who had his own flaws, it was another thing to compete with a dead person who no longer had flaws or whom he had never met.

I was lucky. Brad intuitively knew how to maneuver through my emotional maze. He knew that there were times when I compared him to Chris. He also knew that Chris's death had become a part of who I was. I was too self-absorbed at the time to realize that Brad was going through his own process. He was deciding whether or not he wanted to be in a relationship with me and my memories. He resolved these issues by asking questions about my relationship with Chris, the things we did together, or the people we knew or met together.

I don't think our relationship could have lasted for as long as it did (or our friendship for as long as it has) if he had been threatened by my relationship with Chris. I would not have been able to be in a relationship (then or now) where I was required to kind of eliminate Chris from my life. I could not do that. I know of some relationships where the surviving partner has had to make these kinds of concessions. I don't understand how these relationships survive. Those kinds of concessions represent the widowed partner saying to his new lover, "OK, I'm willing to hide one part of myself from you." I think that kind of relationship is doomed from the beginning.

Of course, I did make some concessions. Every relationship has to make concessions in order to survive. Brad moved into the apartment where Chris and I had lived. When Brad moved in we bought all new bedroom furniture. But in our living room, there was this wood plaque that Chris and I had engraved that read: "Welcome to our Home . . . Chris and Phill." When I asked Brad if he felt that we should take that down, he said "No." But when some of his friends visited, they thought it was odd that the plaque was still on the mantle. Later Brad and I discussed it, and together decided to take it down. Timing for those changes was important because I don't know how I would have reacted if Brad had made that request right away.

My current partner, Torsten, was more threatened by Chris. He has not experienced this kind of major grief and loss. As a result, there were times when the intensity of my memories of Chris were quite difficult for him. It's important for a person who is a widower to be open with his new partner about the grieving process. This is particularly important if the new partner is a stranger to this kind of grief and loss.

MOVING ON

It's telling him it's OK. It's telling him you'll be OK.

I woke up one morning and I knew that it was time to move. Many people had said to me "You need to get out of that house."

People said I needed to move because they didn't think I could get on with my life as long as I lived in the house where Chris died. They couldn't understand that I actually needed to stay there for a certain period of time. That house was my anchor. That house where Chris and I had lived, and where he had died represented safety, security and familiarity. I believed that my memories lived in that house.

A week after I moved, I returned to the old house. I found that I had no feelings of loss, no ache, no hurt. The empty house didn't even feel familiar. I realized that neither the space, the real estate, the address nor the time spent there made it my home. Nor did my memories live in that house either. I discovered that my memories did not live in that house. They lived inside of me. Wherever I lived, Chris would be there. Wherever I went, my memories would go with me.

The grieving process altered my perceptions about events in Chris's and my relationship. The grief crystallized the relationship between the yin and the yang of our life together. As a result I was able to understand that the difficult things did not diminish the value of our relationship. I also came to appreciate the lessons that I learned from the struggles and the less than perfect experiences. Relationships, particularly gay relationships involve, if not require, struggle. I was able to put the truth of our relationship into focus. The clarity of that focus helped me to see the magic that we had and that provided a kind of relief for me in the aftermath of Chris's death.

Chris continues to be an influence on my life. But in a very different way. He is a part of who I am. A month after Chris died, I was going through our safe, looking over insurance policies and other papers when I came across a letter from Chris. It was addressed to me, with instructions to be opened after his death. In the letter he wrote:

"I commend my memory to the hearts of those who knew me. I am secure that I will be remembered. If a life can be measured, let mine be measured by the warmth of the hearts of those who loved me. By this measure, I have lived a life of great richness. Do not despair. What we were will never die. What we are will never fade away. What we will become is in the hands of forces greater than ourselves."

THE NEW AIDS PARADIGM

It's believing, if you work hard enough, fast enough, long enough, if you can keep him on the cutting edge of treatment; maybe he won't die. It's the anger when he dies anyway. It's the guilt because maybe you didn't work hard enough, fast enough or long enough. It's the hopelessness of knowing even a love as great as yours could not save his life.

My life is very different today than it was the first few years after Chris's death. Today, with help from my little pharmacological friends, I'm planning for my future. It may not happen. But for the first time since this epidemic started I feel optimistic enough to think about, to hope for, to plan a future. I think that's a good thing. I also have these surges of rage. All of this new stuff came too late. All the good news in the world will not bring Chris back.

Some people want to take away all the pain. I understand that impulse, but I think but you have to be careful when you fool with history. Who knows what act of the past was the absolutely essential act that created this chain reaction of events that caused some desirable outcome. Sometimes I imagine this med. student in 1989 reading Chris's obituary and based on that experience he became a researcher and went on to discover the protease (David Ho did study in California after all). Perhaps if that person had not read that obituary, maybe he or she would have gone on to become a plastic surgeon instead. Who knows?

I'M NOT DONE YET

It is chronic. It's not manageable. It's not over! Even after he dies.

There was a period of time during my disease when surviving

was not very important to me. It's not that I wanted to die. It was more that I didn't get the point of living. Furthermore, I wasn't convinced that my efforts would alter the outcome of my survival one way or the other.

Finally, I asked myself, "Are you finished? Have you done the things you were meant to do?" I determined that not only was I not finished, but I hadn't even discovered the things that I am meant to do. The new drugs may not bring Chris back. But I can. Or at least I can keep his spirit alive in my work, in my commitment, in my passion for life, in my ability to live and to move on. I owe that to him and to myself.

> In many places you will sense my presence. For, as all who have gone before me, I am in the wind and the sun and the stars. You will hear my voice in your ear, whispering of my love. And when the jacarandas bloom, I know you will see me in their flowers. I will never be apart from you. I will never leave your heart.

—Chris Brownlie, 1989

Conclusion:
Mental Health Considerations
of Gay Widowers

Michael Shernoff

*And Thetis came to the ships and carried with her the gifts of
Hephaistos. She found her beloved son lying in the arms of
Patroclus crying shrill, and his companions in their numbers
about him mourned.*

—The Iliad, Book 19

The story of Achilles' grief and rage mourning the death of
Patroclus in *The Iliad* is only one story that illustrates throughout
the ages, as long as men have loved other men they have buried
their partners and struggled with how to redefine their lives in the
absence of their most beloved. As gay men and lesbians we have
developed unique ways of living our lives, and similarly have
created uniquely relevant ways to mourn our dead and to continue
our lives after the loss of a partner. "Society offers little opportunity
for the overt expression of grief and bereavement in general, and

Michael Shernoff, MSW, is a psychotherapist in private practice in Manhattan
and can be reached vie e-mail at: mshernoff@aol.com or at his home page:
http://members.aol.com/therapysvc.

[Haworth co-indexing entry note]: "Conclusion: Mental Health Considerations of Gay Widowers."
Shernoff, Michael. Co-published simultaneously in *Journal of Gay & Lesbian Social Services* (The
Haworth Press, Inc.) Vol. 7, No. 2, 1997, pp. 137-155; and: *Gay Widowers: Life After the Death of a
Partner* (ed: Michael Shernoff) The Haworth Press, Inc., 1997, pp. 137-155; and: *Gay Widowers: Life
After the Death of a Partner* (ed: Michael Shernoff) The Harrington Park Press, an imprint of The
Haworth Press, Inc., 1997, pp. 137-155. Single or multiple copies of this article are available for a fee from
The Haworth Document Delivery Service [1-800-342-9678, 9:00 a.m. - 5:00 p.m. (EST). E-mail address:
getinfo@haworth.com].

even less opportunity for gay men. Even as gay men grieve, they are subject to homophobia" (Dane & Miller, 1992, p. 157).

Despite generations of gay men burying their partners and becoming widowers there are numerous questions that remain unanswered and need to be examined. How long does one remain a widower? What is entailed in developing an identity as a gay widower? Is it even desirable or appropriate to have a self-definition that largely revolves around the death of one's most significant other? How does a gay man go about adjusting in healthy and adaptive ways to the trauma of a partner's death? Does he still consider himself a widower even after falling in love with someone new and moving into a new relationship? How does where he is on the continuum of "coming out" and developing a positive gay identity affect his grieving and ultimately resolve his mourning? Is there in fact any resolution to the enormity of this kind of loss?

The above are some of the issues and questions that are examined by the men who so generously share their stories in the preceding pages, and I believe for all gay men who have survived the death of a partner. These, as well as other concerns, form the basis of discussions I have had over the past two years, with widowers both in social situations and those who consult me for psychotherapy, as well as with colleagues who counsel these men. I do not believe there are any hard and fast answers to these questions, but rather individual responses that evolve over the course of time.

An interesting phenomenon that occurred with every contributor to this book is important to note. In soliciting essays I was specific that I did not want stories about the deceased partner, about his dying or that was primarily focused on the relationship that the surviving partner had with the deceased. But in every case, the first draft of the essay was exactly that, my own included. How long ago the partner had died, and whether or not the author was now in another satisfying relationship did not affect the fact that all the initial drafts focused on him, then and what happened. Obviously the writers were still traumatized by the experience and were able to recall it with a clarity and detail as if it were only yesterday.

Each author also described being overwhelmed by the intensity of painful and sad feelings that reemerged as they wrote the essay, no matter how many years ago their partner died. A few even called to complain bitterly about how excruciating it was to write about this topic, and yet how important it felt to do so. Several talented authors had to withdraw from this project for precisely this reason. The ones who persevered, each told me how cathartic it was for them to write the essay, tell his story and consciously struggle with putting the focus on himself. Most likely all people who have buried a spouse remain intimately connected to the deceased and to that relationship long after their conscious mourning has ended. Certainly gay men who survive the death of their partner are no different. This is important to be aware of for anyone interested in what gay widowers go through on their journey towards healing, whether you yourself are a widower, are about to lose your partner, or if you are a mental health professional who finds him or herself in the position of working with gay men who are or are about to become widowers.

As Dane and Miller (1992) point out, "In the last decade an extensive literature has evolved about grief, but until very recently, little or no recognition has been given to the grief of homosexual men who survive the death of a partner or friend. Recent theoretical and clinical attention to AIDS and the special problems of homosexual partners of persons with AIDS has resulted in renewed interest in the needs of survivors in relationships that continue to lack social approval" (p. 155). From my work with gay widowers and from conversations with colleagues who also work with this population, it is clear that there is a need for research into the experiences, needs and efficacy of various forms of mental health interventions in order to identify how best to help these men. There remains much for mental health professionals to learn about clinical work with gay widowers that is alluded to and contained within the rich stories in this collection.

For instance, there is hardly any mention of guilt by any of the authors in this book. Some might suggest that ending a relationship with someone who is dying would be fertile grounds for experiencing guilt. Townsand Price-Spratlen and his partner had ostensibly broken up while his partner was dying, and even so there is no indication in Price-Spratlen's story that he is *or should be* wracked by guilt. His story is also an example of how some gay men conceive of their primary relationship differently than a heterosexual marriage. Price-Spratlen very candidly discusses how his grieving and creating a new life was complicated by the fact that he and his partner had redefined their relationship prior to his moving to a different city in another part of the country. Does this make his pain and loss any less valid or intense than that of the men who were living with their partners at the time that they died?

One understandable characteristic that seems fairly typical to burying one's partner/husband/lover is intense anger, whether it be at the unfairness of life, at God, at the cause of death, at the deceased or just being in the unenviable position of having to pick up the pieces and rebuild a life. When a partner dies, a man has no choice but to become a widower. How actively he accepts or rejects the identity of a widower will determine how he deals with all the anger and other difficult feelings inherent in his moving through the grieving process. Craig Lucas' exquisite howling rage is complete and unapologetic in its fury. Ron Najman describes how a skilled and empathetic therapist helped him to discover and clearly realize how angry he had been with his partner prior to his death. Recognizing that there are numerous good reasons to be angry, expressing and integrating it are essential components of adjusting adaptively to widowerhood. As elaborated upon later in this essay, gay widowers' anger is only fueled by homophobic reactions and insensitivity to their mourning.

WIDOWERHOOD AS AN IDENTITY

Prior to AIDS few young or middle aged gay men knew any other gay men who were widowers. Like most people, they generally formed their impressions of who and what a widower was earlier in life. Perhaps it was an elderly grandparent or other relative whose wife had died. In any case rarely was it a young man in the prime of his life. Those first images of a widower are usually not consistent with the man's self-image. Thus, identifying as a gay widower is very likely complicated by the absence of visible role models who are similar to him.

In many ways being a gay widower parallels the coming out process of accepting and embracing one's own homosexuality. "Even in the most benign circumstances, coming to terms with being gay parallels aspects of a traumatized person's journey to reestablish the belief in a meaningful world" (Schwartzberg, 1996, p. 34). In her pioneering paper on Homosexual Identity Formation, Cass (1979) proposes a six-stage model of development that all individuals move through in order to acquire an identity of "homosexual" fully integrated within the individual's overall concept of self. She discusses the distinction between private (personal) and public (social) aspects of identity, and how the development of private and public homosexual identities are two separate but intimately related processes. These concepts seem to be equally true for a gay man struggling with his identity as a widower. Cass's model is also relevant for gay widowers since it is virtually impossible for gay widowers to separate being gay from being a widower. Where the man is in terms of having developed a gay identity, will help determine how he copes with adapting to losing his partner. Cass describes how the development of a stable homosexual identity (and I would add a stable widower's identity) arises from the interaction between individuals and their environment, which supports points raised further on in this article about the importance of social supports to the process of not becoming debilitated by becoming a widower.

Initially the new condition–being sexually and romantically attracted to people of the same sex or being a grieving widower–is not ego syntonic, which means the individual is not comfortable with and does not embrace these experiences or identities. Thus both conditions must be adapted to and grown into. If a boy or man who is just grappling with his recognition of same sex attractions is given the opportunity to meet other sympathetic and like minded people who he can identify with and who encourage and normalize his feelings of attractions to other boys or men, he is given many of the important and necessary supports to cope with the negative aspects of identifying as a member of a sexual minority. This enables him to grow increasingly comfortable embracing his identity as gay and proceeding in the development of an integrated positive identity as a gay man. Usually this can only occur when there are role models available for the person to identify with and a safe and welcoming community. This is equally true for a gay man struggling with making sense out of life without his deceased partner.

The six stages that Cass describes as being necessary for the development of a positive gay identity are equally relevant to the development of a positive and integrated identity as a gay widower.

While I find that the stage model of development that Cass formulates is a useful conceptual framework, I do not adhere to a stage model of coping as my experience has demonstrated that few people actually follow any predictable stages of facing grief or formulating a key component of their identity like being gay or becoming a widower. While some people may in fact follow these expected patterns, many do not. Most men do not necessarily proceed in their development in a linear fashion, but often the man is experiencing aspects of more than one stage simultaneously, and frequently moves back and forth between stages. What follows is a summary of the stages and a synopsis of the salient characteristics that apply equally to forming an identity as a gay man or as a gay widower.

The first stage is labeled "identity confusion." It is predominated by an immediate personal identity crisis of "who am I," during which time the man needs to manage a state of identity confusion and turmoil. Next comes "identity comparison" during which he experiences feelings of alienation, differentness, and loss of old and familiar structures. This is when he begins to reduce his feelings of alienation by addressing and accepting that this new condition (being gay or a widower) does make him different from most of his peers, family members and society at large. Factors such as geographical and social isolation may heighten the experience of alienation. The individual who feels "I'm the only one in the world like this" will experience intense anguish at this stage. "Identity tolerance" follows and is when he begins to recognize and accept the social, sexual and emotional needs that accompany his new state of being. Often he begins to seek out others like himself in order to reduce the social and emotional isolation that is a hallmark of this period.

If there have been no additional traumatic stressors the man moves into a phase known as "identity acceptance" during which time he continues to increase his contact with other men who are like himself, facilitating acceptance rather than just mere tolerance of his self-image as either gay or a widower. This is when he begins to feel a sense of legitimatization and grows increasingly comfortable accepting the support he receives that validates and normalizes what he is experiencing. As the man continues to integrate his new identity, he will next experience "identity pride." This is when he is hyper aware of dividing the world into those who are like him (gay or a widower), and those who are different from him in that they have not shared his experiences. There is a deepening of his identification with and pride in being a member of a minority community. This is one period during which anger frequently is expressed as the person discards earlier efforts to conceal who he is or what he has gone through. The final stage is "identity synthesis" when he no longer needs to divide the world into "me and them." This is when he realizes that not all people who have experienced what he has gone through will have reacted in ways similar to his own. At this time he integrates his identity as either homosexual or a widower into all other aspects of himself, and the new identity is given the status of being merely one aspect of his self.

The process of acquiring a gay identity inherently includes the loss of heterosexual identity and the resulting privileges of heterosexuality. As Schwartzberg (1996) describes, "accepting being gay is a process of sifting through various ingrained cultural beliefs to determine what remains valuable and what must be discarded because it no longer fits. When successful, this struggle transforms feelings of shame, stigma and self-blame into a greater sense of pride and self-worth" (p. 35). An integral component of developing a positive gay identity includes acknowledging and initially mourning the reality of the losses prior to gaining the ability to discover any of the benefits to be derived from embracing the new gay identity. Similarly the gay widower has also lost something very valuable and intrinsic to his identity, his partner who must be mourned in order to move on with his life. Formerly, a central part of the widower's identity was largely bound up with an external reality, his relationship with his partner who is no longer physically present. The struggle the surviving partner must now face is how to internalize what used to be his most significant external relationship through which he defined himself and to whom he still relates alone internally. This phenomenon accounts for some of the distress that

Winston Wilde, John Longres, Ron Najman and I describe in our essays.

Feeling alone and isolated rarely allows an individual to develop a healthy self-image about being gay. Similarly gay widowers need the support of others who have been through the process and who are further along in their journey of recovery from the devastating loss in order to have hope that the future can in fact be better than the excruciating present. Without this support their trauma is only compounded. In addition they need to have their extended mourning process and resulting social awkwardness accepted by friends and family members who may find themselves uncomfortable with the emotional state that the widower experiences for months and sometimes years following the death of his partner. For some men thinking of themselves as a widower is a transient identity that ends once they feel that their period of acute mourning is over, or they have entered into a new romantic relationship. For other men, being a widower becomes integrated into the totality of their personhood which is the firmest example that they have entered the "identity synthesis" stage that Cass describes as the final stage of positive identity formation.

HOMOPHOBIA AND GAY WIDOWS

One dynamic that is unique to the surviving partner of a same sex relationship is that his or her relationship is not universally recognized, validated and valued. "The heterosexual widow or widower who loses a mate receives a tacit level of social support and condolence. Gay men who have been widowed may be more apt to encounter scorn, ostracism, fear or blame" (Schwartzberg, 1996, p. 36). Thus many gay widowers' mourning is complicated by the fact that theirs is a "disenfranchised grief." Doka (1989) explains the concept of *disenfranchised grief* which occurs when (a) the relationship is not recognized, (b) the loss is not recognized, and (c) the griever is not recognized. These are ordinary experiences for many gay men mourning a friend, lover or community. As Dworkin and Kaufer (1995) correctly note, "all of these factors must be taken into account in redefining the process of grieving and identifying the coping mechanisms and interventions appropriate for responding to the needs of today's gay men" (p. 43).

A gay widower experiences disenfranchised grief when he encounters unsympathetic or homophobic responses to his loss. One reaction to encountering an experience that results in disenfranchised grief is a need to defend the relationship he had with the deceased and attempt to prove the relationship's validity to this other unsympathetic individual, whoever he or she might be. There are two direct consequences to this kind of a reaction. First it distracts the widower from his grieving due to his individualized reactions to the shocking reality of the absence of external validation of his relationship and support for what he is the midst of experiencing both socially and emotionally in the aftermath of his partner's death. Second it delays his moving through his grief. Experiencing disenfranchised grief provides the widower with an incentive to keep his relationship with the deceased active as one way of assuring its reality and centrality to his life as a defense from having the relationship negated.

Siegal and Hoefer (1981) highlight problems such as hostility from families and exclusion from the planning of funeral arrangements, or even from the service itself which are all unique stressors that a gay man may be forced to face immediately after the death of his partner. Even a gay man who is completely open in all areas of his life about being gay may experience homophobic reactions following the death of his partner. For example, it is not unusual for a gay man to be denied the same bereavement leave from his place of business that any heterosexually married individual normally receives. In addition, the surviving partner may not receive condolences from family or workers who do not view a gay relationship as the equivalent of a marriage.

The Cass model of gay identity formation is one useful way to conceptualize the various phases that gay widowers go through following the death of their partner. It is also an important window through which to understand what happens when the trauma of losing one's partner reawakens previously resolved internalized homophobic feelings about being gay. The absence of normal supportive and compassionate responses from family, friends and coworkers can trigger shame in some gay widowers. If the man is unable to recognize that his shame reaction is a denial of the validity of his own angry and hurt feelings, he is often taken back to a less developed stage of gay identity formation by denying the enormity of his loss and what the deceased meant to him.

"With their experience of repeated loss, gay survivors often have to struggle against being identified as blameworthy" (Dane & Miller, 1992, p. 158). For gay widowers who have grown up in very conservative or fundamentalist religious families, the absence of family support and nurturance during the period of acute grief often has the potential to trigger feelings of internalized homophobia that may have been quiescent for years. One way this plays out is in feeling somehow that they did something to deserve the pain they are in the midst of experiencing. Another way blame is internalized and becomes merged with homophobia is in thinking if "I were not gay perhaps then I would not be feeling this way." It is obviously true that if the man were not gay he would not have fallen in love with the other man who died and who he is now mourning. The problem in this line of thinking is that it merges being gay with the pain, which is an indication of the old internalized homophobia, rather than the pain is an appropriate response to having loved and lost the beloved. If a survivor is HIV positive, and his partner died from AIDS, the concept of being "blameworthy" can complicate his bereavement as he struggles with "Why am I still alive while my spouse died from this disease?"

AIDS AND BEREAVEMENT

Obviously gay men have endured widowerhood long before AIDS. But the current health crisis has brought an urgency and focus to the issue of gay men surviving the death of a partner due to "the increasing number of deaths by AIDS among gay men that has resulted in an increasing number of survivors who confront the effects of grief and bereavement" (Dane & Miller, 1992, pp. 155-156). As Dworkin and Kaufer (1995) note "The bereavement process experienced by gays and lesbians who experience losses due to HIV/AIDS must be understood as a chronic state of mourning. The implications of overlapping losses where the onset of mourning for one loss overlaps with the end stage of mourning for another loss are significant. Complicating this chronic state are post-traumatic stress, loss saturation, unresolved grief, survivor guilt, and fear of infection with HIV" (p. 42). Dean et al. (1988) stress that not only are gay men losing those with whom they have shared strong emotional ties, but they are also losing acquaintances, role models and co-workers at a very fast rate. Thus individual clinicians have to be prepared to assume a role of support and bearing witness that transcends traditional psychotherapy or counseling. The experience of many urban gay men is similar to that of a survivor of a major catastrophe, and must be addressed with this understanding and within this context.

TRAUMA THEORY AND GAY WIDOWERS

Gabriel (1996) states that "PWAs are emerging as the newest group of persons experiencing psychological trauma" (p. 6). While in agreement with this statement I would only add that surviving partners almost all demonstrate symptoms of emotional and psychological trauma during the demise of and following the death of their partner. Gabriel cites Bonnie Green (1990) as listing exposure to the grotesque, violent/sudden loss of a loved one and learning of exposure to a noxious agent causing death or severe harm to another as two events that are considered trauma-inducing. As Gabriel (1996) notes "AIDS survivors can quickly attest to the presence of these elements in varying degrees of intensity in their everyday lives" (p. 6). Given the nature and dimensions of traumatic stress, having a partner die of any cause constitutes a traumatic event, and needs to be clinically addressed within this context by mental health professionals working with a gay widower.

Gabriel (1996) summarizes the research on trauma survivors which suggests survivors of trauma exhibit a cluster of uniform responses. A common denominator of all psychological trauma according to Herman (1992) is "a feeling of intense fear, helplessness, loss of control and threat of annihilation" (p. 33). Most of the widowers I have known both socially and professionally have exhibited many of these reactions, and thus surviving the death of a partner needs to be recognized diagnostically as the trauma it is, and responded to clinically with appropriate interventions. Among the signs of turmoil Gabriel (1996) lists that surviving partners may exhibit are distressing emotional reactions such as anxiety, dread, horror, fear, rage, shame, sadness and depression; intrusive imagery of dying; nightmares; flashbacks of images of the stressor; numbing or avoidance of a situation associated with the images; somatic complaints including sleep difficulties; substance abuse; impaired social functioning; interpersonal difficulties; sexual dysfunction, hyper sexuality and difficulty sustaining intimate relationships.

My clinical and social experience confirms that most gay widowers experience some combination of these symptoms, thus supporting the concept that they are trauma survivors. "The inability to escape mental reminders of a trauma is one of the symptoms of post-traumatic stress disorder (PTSD). At times the survivors are bombarded with 'intrusive thoughts'–painful fragments of the trauma that intrude, unwanted into regular consciousness" (Schwartz-berg, 1996, p. 116). With the previous explanation, Schwartzberg provides the conceptual framework for understanding the difficulty so many of the authors had in working on their essays for this book. Citing Horowitz (1976), Schwartzberg notes that traumatized individuals often experience a "cycle of intrusion and denial" (p. 116) in their continuing efforts to recover from trauma. As I mentioned at the beginning of this essay, each of the men who contributed to this book maintains a vivid and intense memory of the final illness, death and time immediately following the death of his partner, even now many years later. Experiencing vivid recall of a traumatic event is one classic symptom seen in most trauma survivors.

THE IMPORTANCE OF COMMUNITY SUPPORTS

Dworkin and Kaufer (1995) suggest that bereavement interventions also need to respond to developmental issues, existential themes, multiple and chronic primary and secondary losses, and the collective nature of grieving. They must be gay affirmative in addressing lowered self-esteem, personal identity and questions about body image, and need to address the reestablishment of meaning in one's life. Many authors cited by Dworkin and Kaufer (1995) emphasize that social support is the key to coping with any loss, especially multiple loss. Yet with many entire friendship networks being wiped out by AIDS, the therapist, group leader and grief support group members all are challenged to assume a role and significance that may be a combination of counselor, friend, significant other and just fellow human being. For the surviving partner, weekly therapy or group sessions may be the only remaining ongoing regular contact with any individual with whom he has a history.

Figley (1986) has found that an inadequate support system can contribute to the development of a traumatic stress reaction. This absence of understanding and support only increases the pain and anger surrounding a widower's loss, and has the potential to exacerbate whatever symptoms of psychological trauma the surviving partner may already be experiencing, as George Seabold's story poignantly illustrates. All mental health professionals doing individual or group counseling must be aware of these additional issues which have an impact upon a gay man's grieving process, and find ways to elicit feelings of anger and shame that may surface in the absence of appropriate support, reframe these experiences and actively console the grieving partner.

Seabold's descent into active alcoholism following the death of his partner is but one clear example of the cost of grieving in isolation without any of the needed social and emotional supports during this difficult transitional time. John Longres, Ron Najman and Don Bachardy all describe the innumerable benefits derived from supportive friends and families. With George Seabold's story as an example, it is important to note that men who are currently in recovery from alcoholism and/or drug addiction are at higher risk of relapsing into use of alcohol and/or drugs following the death of their partner. Men in recovery need to be encouraged to go to meetings, actively work their program and strengthen their connections to other people in the program during this particularly stressful period in their lives.

DEPRESSION, NORMAL AND PATHOLOGICAL GRIEF

Any grieving individual is at heightened risk for lapsing into a serious depression if his expressions of grief and rage are not supported and facilitated by friends and empathic professionals. If the man has a history of depression prior to the death of his partner and is not currently on anti-depressant medication it is useful for both the widower and the therapist to be on the lookout for any indications that a clinical depression may be setting in. At the first indications of the onset of clinical depression the man should be referred to a psychopharmacologist (who is a psychiatrist who specializes in prescribing psychotropic drugs) for a medication evaluation. A pathological level of depressive reaction to the death of a partner must be differentiated from the understandable profound sadness and unhappiness that is a natural reaction to the loss. Symptoms of a pathological grief reaction or depression precipitated by the death of a partner are: isolating one's self from loving and supportive people; not returning phone calls, e-mail or answering the door when someone comes to visit; hopelessness that life ever will again be better than it now is; remaining in bed; not going to work; a preoccupation with wanting to join the deceased; a sense of the meaninglessness of life without the deceased; and thoughts of wanting to die now that the lover is gone. Many of the above symptoms are normal components of a healthy grieving process but only if they are transitory and not indications of the individual becoming incapacitated or obsessed with thoughts about the dead partner.

Gay widowers often suffer from depression that is combined with and exacerbated by a sense that their lives have lost its meaning. Schwartzberg (1996) states that depression and meaninglessness often go hand in hand. "People who are depressed find little meaning in life, and one can lead to the other" (p. 118). He goes on to differentiate between depression and meaninglessness by stating that depression has specific symptoms (which can often be treated). "Meaninglessness is broader–both more encompassing and more diffuse. Depression has at its heart an acute sense of loss; meaninglessness speaks more to emptiness, purposelessness, and disillusionment. An underlying question of severe depression is 'How can I live in such pain?' With severe meaninglessness, the question instead is, 'Why bother living, what's the point?' " (Schwartzberg, 1996, p. 118). Clearly widowers suffer from a crisis of meaning in their lives following the death of their partner, and one of the indications that they are recovering from the trauma of their loss is when the surviving partner begins to rediscover and recreate meaning in his profoundly changed life.

MOVING ON

Most of what I have learned during my journey from a newly bereaved man to where I am now, further along, is that there is no one, correct path. The death of a partner is often the reason why people begin psychotherapy or counseling, as both Winston Wilde and Ron Najman discuss in their essays. But it is important to remember that traditional psychotherapy is by no means the only useful or appropriate way that professionals can be of assistance during this period following the death of a partner. Referring gay widowers to a gay specific bereavement group is often one helpful intervention in assisting the surviving partner to work through his grief. Yet as John Longres discovered, a bereavement group may not be of help if the match between the leader's style and the needs of the widower are not congruent.

Many men find that their need to continue to talk about their evolution and pain is more than their friends can tolerate. Even loving and sympathetic friends may not be enough to help a man through this process. If this is the case, this is usually a good time for the widower to think about talking with a professional skilled in working with gay men who have lost a partner. Widowers frequently arrive in my office with very intact friendship groups and supportive families, but say "I'm afraid that I'm wearing my friends out and that they simply don't want to hear me go on about my grieving any more." In many cases these men are correct. Grieving and reconstructing a life are by no means on any predetermined time table or schedule, and as previously mentioned may continue for years.

Gabriel (1996) reports that studies of survivor groups (Danieli, 1985; Lindy, 1988; Herman, 1992) suggest that the response of the larger community, outside of the kinship group, is also a source of an important connection for those surviving a traumatic experience. When the surviving partner is a member of a sexual minority which is denied visibility, his trauma is only exacerbated, which is why it is crucial that there be supportive structures in place for gay widowers within the gay and lesbian community. Herman (1992) has found that such a community response in the face of a traumatic event has the potential to be of enormous assistance in helping repair the injury inflicted by the traumatic event.

Many cities now have bereavement programs geared specifically for gay men who have lost a loved one to AIDS run by one of the lesbian or gay social service agencies or AIDS bereavement groups conducted by hospitals in hard-hit communities. Yet gay specific bereavement groups also need to be developed for individuals whose partners have died from a cause other than AIDS. One of the prime tasks of the counselor, therapist or group members is to bear witness and hear the stories of the survivor while at the same time offering faith and hope for a future that is less filled with pain.

CONCLUSION

Invariably, each widower ponders, am I doing this correctly? As the stories in this book reveal, there is no right or wrong way to go about the process of moving on after the death of a partner. Perhaps the only incorrect thing to do is to try to avoid the painful feelings that must be experienced in order to come out the other side. In our society there are powerful cultural myths, usually unspoken, about how to mourn "correctly." "These myths touch on many aspects of grieving–how long to mourn, what to feel, what not to feel, how to behave, how not to behave, when to show certain responses, with whom to share your feelings, and so on. Mourners face many implicit directives about how to conduct their grief" (Schwartzberg, 1996, p. 167).

Schwartzberg (1996) also notes that the myths pertaining to how to grieve correctly are not always true. Wortman and Silver (1989) suggest that many of our most basic, unquestioned assumptions about how people cope with loss may not match people's actual experience. Among the assumptions that they question are: (1) Is depression an inevitable consequence of loss? (2) Does the absence of depression indicate a pathological response? and (3) Do all significant losses need to be "worked through" in order to be healed? Although I agree with their overall premise, I do not agree that not all significant losses need to be worked through in order to be healed. What is open to examination is what constitutes "working through." I believe that there are an infinite variety of forms that the working through may take, none being better or worse, if they are adaptive to the individual's healing. But both my clinical and personal experience demonstrate the necessity of resolving or making accommodations to a traumatic life event, in order to not be continuously crippled by it.

Schwartzberg (1996) explains that in western culture many people follow a similar path in grieving a major loss. The individual responds with depression and pain for a discrete period that can last upwards to a couple of years, and then gradually returns to his previous level of functioning. He notes that a sizable minority do not follow this path. I believe that the stories in this book are examples of a variety of individualized reactions to the death of one's partner which supports Schwartzberg's contention about the multiplicity of ways that people may grieve.

Schwartzberg also states that some people have a very prolonged reaction, like that described by George Seabold and Phill Wilson in their chapters. Other people have a very abbreviated grief reaction, regaining full momentum of their lives quickly. He cautions that to react differently from the cultural norm, by grieving too long, for example, or too little, needn't mean that a response is unhealthy. "People vary greatly in how they respond to a significant life upheaval; the absence of turmoil may simply reflect another style of 'normal' response" (Schwartzberg, 1996, p. 168).

"For most bereaved people, to keep going after the painful life changes caused by death is the most difficult task of all. When a lover dies, the loss plunges the bereaved person into a world where many of his known and habitual structures of daily life disappear into a world more full of confusion, disorganization and anxiety than it was prior to the death of his partner. A new order has to be constructed" (Dane & Miller, 1992, p. 171). The men whose stories are told in this book each provide a sterling example of hope and triumph in their ability to surmount the pain and trauma of the loss of their partner and continue on with their lives in new and meaningful ways. Surviving the death of a partner is a potentially devastating emotional experience. "Yet some people emerge from their grieving process with unexpected gains. By weathering emotional tribulations they had thought unendurable, they have a deeper, surer sense of their strength. By facing despair, and not succumbing, they know their inner capacities in a more complete way. These gains do not in any way diminish the fact of the loss. But yes, they are benefits. Dearly purchased, hard-earned benefits" (Schwartzberg, 1996, p. 82).

Ultimately widowerhood is a period simultaneously of crisis and of resolution. It is a time of transition and reflection on both the past as well as the future, and a time for sowing the seeds for new beginnings. Often it is full of new, exhausting, and potentially thrilling challenges. It can be a period for rediscovering and possibly reinventing one's self or at least certain facets of one's life. Listening to widowers describe their journeys, and as I reflect on my own path since Lee's death, I am often reminded of the myth of the Phoenix which is reborn out of its own ashes. As the stories in this book demonstrate, survival, experimenting first with a different sense of oneself as a person now alone and then with countless possibilities, new relationships, and innovative directions in life, all have the possibility of creating something fresh and unforeseen that can emerge out of the ashes of the death of a beloved partner.

REFERENCES

Cass, V. (1979). Homosexual identity formation: A theoretical model. *Journal of Homosexuality, 4*(3), 219-235.

Dane, B., & Miller S. (1992). *AIDS: Intervening with hidden grievers.* Westport, CT: Auburn House.

Danieli, Y. (1985). The treatment and prevention of long term effects and intergenerational transmission of victimization: A lesson from Holocaust survivors. In C. Figley (Ed.), *Trauma and its wake: The study and treatment of post-traumatic stress disorder* (pp. 295-98). New York: Brunner/Mazel.

Dean, L., Hall, W., & Martin, J. (1988). Chronic and intermittent AIDS-related bereavement in a panel of homosexual men in New York City. *Journal of Palliative Care, 4*(4), 54-57.

Doka, K. (1989). *Disenfranchised grief: Recognizing hidden sorrow.* Lexington, MA: Lexington Books.

Dworkin, J., & Kaufer, D. (1995). Social services and bereavement in the gay and lesbian community. In G. Lloyd & M.A. Kuszelewicz (Eds.), *HIV disease: Lesbians, gays and the social services* (pp. 41-60). New York: The Harrington Park Press.

Figley, C. (1986). Traumatic stress: The role of the family and social support system. In C. Figley (Ed.), *Trauma and its wake: The study and treatment of post-traumatic stress disorder* (pp. 39-58). New York: Brunner/Mazel.

Gabriel, M. (1996). *AIDS trauma and support group therapy.* New York: The Free Press.

Green, B. (1990). Defining trauma: Terminology and generic stressor dimensions. *Journal of Applied Social Psychology, 20*(20), 1632-42.

Herman, J. (1992). *Trauma and recovery.* New York: Basic Books.

Horowitz, M. (1976). *Stress response syndromes.* New York: Aronson.

Schwartzberg, S. (1996). *A crisis of meaning: How gay men are making sense of AIDS.* New York: Oxford University Press.

Siegal, R., & Hoefer, D. (1981). Bereavement counseling for gay individuals. *American Journal of Psychotherapy, 35* (4), 517-525.

Wortman, C.B., & Silver, R.C. (1989). The myths of coping. *Journal of Consulting and Clinical Psychology, 57*, 349-357.

Index

Abuse, sexual, feelings following, 78-79
Acquired immunodeficiency syndrome. *See* AIDS
ADODI, 61,65-66,67
ADODI IBAYE, 67
AIDS, 77,120
    dementia and, xv
    mourning process and, 146-147
AIDS survivors, 147
Alcoholics Anonymous (AA), 13
Alcoholism, 10-14,86-87,149
Alechim, S., 22
Amen-Ra, 68
Anger, 78,140
Anniversaries, 45
    effects of, on surviving partners, 25-26
    mourning process and, 88-89

Bachardy, D., 4,101-111,149
Beam, J., 67
Belle, R., 70
Bereavement groups, 151-152
Bereavement process. *See* Mourning process
Birthdays, 89
Bonding, 20-28
"Brotherhood of the survivors," 66
Brownlie, C., 125-136
Burial arrangements, 10

Careers
    effect of partner's death on, 17-19
    ending relationships for, 62

following partner's death, 120-123
    as havens, 116
    as solace for grief, 10
Cass, V., 141,142,144,145-146
Child abuse, remembering, following partner's death, 78-79
Churches, 9, 10-11
Cirrhosis of the liver, 84,87
Clayborne, J. L., 83-100
Closet
    lifestyles while in, 8-9
    survival of partner while in, 7-14
Closure, for surviving partners, 28
Community supports, importance of, 148-149
Coping, with terminal illness of partner, 9-10
Counselors, grief, 55
Crying, 117

Dane, B., 139,146,153
Danieli, Y., 151
Dating, following partner's death, 11, 20-28,34,35,50-52,105, 131-133
Dean, L., 147
Death. *See also* Partner's death
    finality of, 16
    moment of partner's, 16
    as process, xvii
    waiting for, 15-16
Delany, S. R., 67
Dementia, xv
Depression, 149-150
Diaries, use of, following partner's death, 103-104